Discovering Fire

Haiku & Essays

DAVID GRAYSON

Discovering Fire: Haiku & Essays

Published by
Red Moon Press
P. O. Box 2461
Winchester VA
22604-1661 USA
www.redmoonpress.com

ISBN 978-1-936848-59-1

First printing

For Lynn, Miles, and Audrey

In memory of
Philip Grayson, 1926–2010

TABLE OF CONTENTS

I. Essays: Haiku Practice

The Sword of Cliché: Choosing a Topic ... 9
Word Choice in English-Language Haiku:
    The Uses of Roots ... 17
Word Choice in English-Language Haiku:
    The Uses of Foreign Words ... 25
Writing Haiku: The Two-Line Form ... 35
The Twin Pleasures of *Kigo* ... 45
Leaping Haiku ... 47

II. Haiku and Senryu

III. Essays: Haiku Poets

Beyond the Trailhead:
    Laurie Stoelting's Haiku ... 55
The Trickster: An Introduction
    to Patrick Gallagher's Haiku ... 61
J. D. Salinger and Haiku ... 65
The Half-Finished Bridge: Rich Krivcher,
    Tanya McDonald, Linda Papanicolaou,
    Joseph Robello ... 71
Moonlight Changing Direction: Fay Aoyagi,
    Christopher Herold, John Stevenson,
    Billie Wilson ... 77

IV. Haiku and Senryu

V. Essays: Haiku and Art

The "Ancient Enemy": Death in Art
and Haiku ... 87
Glossy Black Painting: Notes on Modern Art
and Haiku ... 95
"The Inspiration of a Moment": Calder's Mobiles
and Haiku ... 97
Simple Ingredients: *New Yorker* Cover Art
and Haiku ... 103

VI. Haiku and Senryu

VII. Essays: Haiku and Religion

Notes on Taoism and Haiku ... 111
Unity ... 115
Mystery ... 119
Grace ... 121
Ritual ... 123
Haiku as Prayer ... 127

VIII. Haiku and Senryu

IX. Essays: The Short Poem

The Eye of the Storm: Micropoems ... 135
Short Poems: Nothing to Take Away ... 151

Discovering Fire

The Sword of Cliché: Choosing a Topic

I currently live in Alameda, a Bay Area town situated next to Oakland and directly across the bay from San Francisco. I'm married and a parent. I work for an Internet company in San Francisco. My life revolves around family, work, and friends. Like many haiku poets, the bricks-and-mortar of my daily life are also the bricks-and-mortar of my haiku.

However, residing in a dense urban environment layers another set of topics onto my haiku. The characteristics of life in a large metropolitan area constitute some of the oxygen of my daily life, and naturally my writing. Wealth and poverty, social and ethnic diversity, traffic and crime, restaurants and cultural pursuits, open space and architecture are all threads in the fabric of my daily life. Not surprisingly, these realities too are recurring preoccupations of my haiku.

> the coldness
> of my pocket change—
> cardboard shelter[1]

1. 3rd Place, 2008 Anita Sadler Weiss Awards.; in *A New Resonance 6: Emerging Voices in English-Language Haiku*, eds. Jim Kacian and Dee Evetts. Winchester, VA: Red Moon Press, 2009, 53.

One topic that I find myself returning to often is homelessness. For a haiku writer (indeed, for any artist) the choice of a topic for a poem usually feels natural and "organic." Any topic that arises directly from experience is bound to feel legitimate.

However, a writer needs to be on guard against the risks that attend certain topics — not the least of which is cliché. A cliché is an idea that has been overused to the point that it has lost its original force or novelty. Of course, sometimes it is not the topic itself that leads to cliché but rather how a writer handles it. At the same time, experienced writers know that certain subjects carry a greater risk.

From my perspective, homelessness is one such topic. On the one hand, avoiding it seems absurd. I encounter homeless men and women every day. Sometimes, the circumstance of homelessness is unique or particularly jarring. For example, I once encountered a mother begging for money while her son—who was close in age to my own then-five-year-old—played next to her. In another example, I was confronted with the overpowering smell of a wheelchair-bound man who had defecated in his pants and was struggling to clean himself in full public view, while an attending police officer stood off to the side, hesitant to begin helping him. Many urban residents share similar experiences, including Paul Mena:

scattering pigeons—
a homeless man
flirts with schoolgirls[2]

It would be nonsensical for me to consciously avoid the topic. On the other hand, the topic of homelessness is fraught with pitfalls. First, the act of simply choosing this topic may trigger skepticism. I may be subject to "political" challenges: what right do I, who am not homeless, have to write about the subject? Will my work necessarily treat the homeless as objects, however well-meaning my intentions? For instance, am I focusing only on the most visible slice of the homeless population (those living on the street, often mentally ill)? Finally, if I am construed as merely an observer, or only incidentally a participant, there is the charge that the haiku is not based on direct experience—it is almost a desk-ku.

Beyond these arguments, I face the challenge of writing a poem that meets the standard of previous admired work or offers new insight. It is all too easy to succumb to the cluster of emotions that is typically evoked with this topic: indignation, pity, hyperbole, and so forth are all (understandably) easy emotional responses to fall into.

2. Paul David Mena, *Simply Haiku*. 1:6 <http://www.poetrylives.com/SimplyHaiku/SHvin6/Paul_Mena_haiku.html>. Accessed March 28, 2010.

Because the topic is inherently sensitive, the writer may be in danger of writing a less good poem. That is, because of its inherent nature, the topic can do much of the work for the writer; it can trigger a powerful response in a reader even if the poem is not great. Put another way, it's probably easier to write a mediocre haiku about homelessness than a mediocre haiku about, say, traffic congestion. The subject of homelessness itself does a lot of the "heavy lifting" for the writer.

So, the writer—to use a cliché—is stuck between a rock and a hard place. The subjects that are often the most compelling are precisely those that have been written about before—and remembered by readers. These subjects inherently encourage the writer to fall under the spell of a timeworn response—to fall on the sword of cliché. However, it is essential to remember that each of these risks also offers opportunity.

As Paul Williams noted, good haiku usually stem from our daily lives: "such perceptions as do transform themselves into haiku tend to emerge from the familiar rather than the new."[3] Repetition affords the writer the opportunity to reflect and see a subject from many different angles. This

---

3. Paul O. Williams, "Loafing Alertly: Observation and Haiku," in *The Nick of Time: Essays on Haiku Aesthetics*, eds. Lee Gurga and Michael Dylan Welch. Foster City, CA: Press Here, 2001, 21.

can help the writer move beyond commonplace observations and achieve a more nuanced or unique understanding.

> As the month ends . . .
>> the line at the soup kitchen
>>> longer every day . . .[4]

In this poem, Tom Tico notices the subtle changes that occur over time at the soup kitchen. This is not a one-time impression.

> homeless guy
> the santa hat finally
> in season[5]

The same dynamic is present in this haiku by Roberta Beary. It's clear that the poet has encountered this person before, and this fact forms the basis for her observation. In both Tico's and Beary's haiku, a long-standing familiarity with the subject matter provides the foundation for the poem.

A writer should certainly be concerned about portraying a subject (homeless or otherwise) as an object or a "prop" for their own ideas or ends.

4. Tom Tico, *Spring Morning Sun*. San Francisco: Belltower Press, 1998, 68.
5. Roberta Beary, Shiki Monthly Kukai—November 2008. <http://www. haikuworld.org/kukai/recent.nov08.html>. Accessed October 16, 2010.

However, it is often true that topics like these stimulate the writer in unplanned and surprising ways. Robert Spiess noted: "In the better haiku there is a surprisingly large amount of subjectivity beneath the objectivity of the haiku's entities ... It is this subjective aspect that accounts for very much of the difference between a haiku that is merely descriptive per se and one that engenders intuitional feeling . . ."[6]

> homeless beggar—
> the itch of his clothes
> all down my spine[7]

In this poem by H. F. Noyes, the "homeless beggar" is the initial focus of attention. But in the last two lines, the focus shifts to the speaker. Although this shift away from the beggar may seem self-centered, it is in fact this subjective response that conveys the empathy. The speaker imagines—strongly, viscerally—what it might feel like to be the homeless beggar.

---

6. Robert Spiess, *A Year's Speculations on Haiku*. Madison, Wisconsin: Modern Haiku Press, 1995, 16.
7. H. F. Noyes, in *The Red Moon Anthology 1996: The Best English-Language Haiku of the Year*, ed. Jim Kacian. Winchester, VA: Red Moon Press, 1997, 81.

homeless man
the postman delivers
a smile[8]

The same is true in Elena Naskova's poem. The homeless subject is the first image, but the main character is the postman. It is the postman's subjective response—his smile—that calls attention to the humanity of the homeless man, who might be overlooked by others.

In each of these cases, the poet waded into tricky territory and returned not with a heavy-handed gesture but with a fresh insight. Venturing into such subject areas is challenging, but it offers rewards for those who learn how to step carefully.

---

8. Elena Naskova, Shiki Monthly Kukai—November 2008. <http://www. haikuworld.org/kukai/recent.nov08.html>. Accessed October 16, 2010.

Word Choice in English-Language Haiku:
The Uses of Roots

morning shower—
finding just the word
I was looking for
　　—Carolyn Hall[1]

W ord choice stands at the center of the practice of writing. This is particularly true for poetry, and even more so for haiku. Simply put, the choice of a word can make or break a poem. Choosing the right word entails a myriad of considerations. Etymology can be a useful part of this process: Words originating in different periods have different properties and reflect unique states.

For English-language haiku poets, a useful starting point is distinguishing Anglo-Saxon (Old English) words from those descended from Latin (Middle English). It's estimated that half of the commonly used words today have Old English roots.[2] These words are older and often shorter, and contain few syllables. Typically they include the first words that native speakers learn as children: *good, bad, hot, cold, eat, sleep,* and so forth. As such,

1. Carolyn Hall, *Water Lines: Haiku and Senryu*, ed. John Barlow. Liverpool: Snapshot Press, 2006, 20.
2. *EnglishClub*, retrieved October 5, 2012 from http://www.englishclub.com/ english-language-history.htm.

they possess a strong visceral resonance. When you compare these words with their Latin-derived synonyms, the differences are readily apparent:

Old English	*Middle English*
eat	consume
dead	deceased
dog	canine
rain	precipitation

The Old English-descended words are simpler and more direct, imagistic, and colloquial.

> first frost
> the echo in the caw
> of the crow[3]

Mark Hollingsworth's poem (which won *Frogpond*'s best of the Fall 2009 issue) contains the Old English-derived words "first," "frost," and "crow." These words produce an austere and spare feeling that underscores the scene.

> the sack of kittens
> sinking in the icy creek,
> increases the cold[4]

---

3. Mark Hollingsworth, *Frogpond* 32:3, 29.
4. Nicholas Virgilio. In *The Haiku Anthology*, ed. Cor van den Heuvel. New York: W. W. Norton & Company, 1999, 259.

In this classic by Nick Virgilio, the Old English words—"sack," "sink," "creek," and "cold"—paint a sharp picture that is multi-sensory. The reader can feel the cold and the wet, and imagine the muffled cries of the kittens.

As is apparent in these two examples, Anglo-Saxon words offer several benefits. Because they are more visual, they can better evoke a scene. Because they are shorter, not only can they be accommodated in haiku, they can actually contribute to the compression of the poem. Additionally, Anglo-Saxon lends itself to alliteration; in fact, alliteration was a notable attribute of Old English literature.

In contrast, Latin-derived vocabulary from Middle English tends to be used in formal communication. It predominates in scientific and medical terminology, as well as in the legal and academic fields. Some writers and teachers recommend avoiding Latinate terms altogether because the vocabulary has been used to remove "subjectivity" from prose.

But a wholesale rejection of Middle English is unwarranted. This vocabulary is an indispensable part of everyday English. Sometimes it makes better sense to use a Latin-derived word.

sunflowers
the tube of cadmium yellow
squeezed flat[5]

Claire Gallagher's poem is comprised of rich words, but I think that "cadmium" is the key one. "Cadmium" is from the Latin *cadmia*, itself from the earlier Greek *kadmeia*.[6] The word has a complex set of sounds. It's unusual and stands out, granting uniqueness to the poem.

abracadabra—
the hairy tarantula
waves his arms at me[7]

There are two key words in this haiku by Patricia Machmiller. The word "tarantula" is of Latin origin and is a relatively recent addition to English, from the sixteenth century.[8] The second word, "abracadabra," is also Latin-derived. The poem is playful and unnerving at the same time, and both words fit the mood.

5. Haiku Poets of Northern California, retrieved October 5, 2012 from http://www.hpnc.org/past-contests/2004-haiku-senryu-tanka-rengay-contests-result.
6. Merriam-Webster, retrieved October 5, 2012 from http://www.merriam-webster.com/dictionary/cadmium.
7. Patricia J. Machmiller. In *San Francisco Bay Area Nature Guide and Saijiki*, eds. Anne M. Homan, Patrick Gallagher & Patricia J. Machmiller. San Jose: Yuki Teikei Haiku Society, 2010, 64.
8. Ibid.

These distinctions also play out with *kigo*, or season words. The effectiveness of a *kigo* is based not only on its meaning and history but also its sound. As mentioned above, the formal scientific terms are typically Latin-based, while the common usage is from Old English. Poets of course largely use the common terms, but occasionally the rarer form makes sense, as in this Kiyoko Tokutomi poem translated by Fay Aoyagi and Patricia Machmiller:

> Where my mother lives
> standing there
> towering cumulus[9]

The word "cumulus" is bigger (that is, longer) than the alternative "cloud" and evokes the expansive setting and "towering" body. "Cumulus" is also more open-ended than "cloud," which is short and ends with a hard "d" sound. The translators' choice better matches the wistful and meditative mood of the poem.

It's useful to remember that the Anglo-Saxon vs. Latin dichotomy is not always cut-and-dried, however. Sometimes, a word can surprise you, as in Gary Snyder's poem:

---

9. Kiyoko Tokutomi, *Kiyoko's Sky: The Haiku of Kiyoku Tokutomi*. Trans. Fay Aoyagi & Patricia Machmiller. Decatur, IL: Brooks Books, 2002.

Pissing

watching

a

waterfall

(*the Tokugawa Gorge*)[10]

Without resorting to the dictionary, we might reasonably assume that "piss" (vs. "urinate") would be of older lineage in English. It denotes a basic bodily function, is one syllable, and is of common (even vulgar) usage. But it's of Latin (French) origin. So, there are exceptions.

Awareness of etymology can be a useful guide to finding the right word or confirming why one does work so well. It is as useful for non-native speakers of English as much as for those for whom it is their mother tongue. Of course, English is a wonderfully layered and still-evolving language. But knowledge of its Anglo-Saxon and Latin foundations is essential, even if—as Carolyn Hall observes—we don't always alight on the perfect word:

---

10. American Haiku Archives, retrieved October 5, 2012 from http://www.americanhaikuarchives.org/curators/GarySynder.html.

autumn dusk —
a word that will do
for the one I can't find[11]

11. Carolyn Hall, *How to Paint the Finch's Song*. Winchester, VA: Red Moon Press, 2010.

WORD CHOICE IN ENGLISH-LANGUAGE HAIKU: THE USES OF FOREIGN WORDS

As befits such a short form, word choice is of capital importance in haiku. As a haiku poet explores the best words for a poem, it's not surprising that occasionally he or she will land upon a non-English word. Sometimes a poet will determine that a foreign word better conveys the intended meaning than an English one, or perhaps adds an association that English cannot. In a world where cross-fertilization between languages is commonplace, haiku poets can turn to an expanded poetic "inventory" to create their work.

Not surprisingly, one topic in which other languages are used is travel. These two haiku, from the quartet "Four Rome Haiku" by Dietmar Tauchner, are examples:

> *curia*
> the constant chatter
> of tourist tongues

> a downpour
> cleans the *via del corso*
> of people[1]

---

1. Dietmar Tauchner, from "Four Rome Haiku," in *Modern Haiku* 41.1 (winter-spring 2010), 86.

The Italian words in these haiku instantly transport the reader to the city of Rome. It's important to note that the words that Tauchner chooses to retain in Italian are Italian-specific. The *Via del Corso* is a historic thoroughfare in central Rome; *curia* refers to the organization of the Vatican. These unique local terms help draw the reader into the experience.

> Ash Wednesday—
> carrying a *retablo*
> through the pelting rain[2]

In this poem by Patricia Machmiller, the word *retablo* (a Latin American term referring to a small religious painting, often used in home altars)[3] roots the haiku in a place. It evokes a cultural event for the reader. If Machmiller had substituted an English word for the original Spanish, the haiku would not be as effective. A close equivalent in English ("reredos") is derived from the Latin and is too formal; there is no colloquial counterpart. A more informal phrase, for instance "religious altar painting," would be unwieldy.

In all three examples, it's clear how important <u>sound is in the experience</u> of a poem. These words

2. Patricia Machmiller, in *Mariposa* 10 (Spring/Summer 2004), 7.
3. Ibid. Machmiller defines "retablo" as "Mexican folk art. A small religious painting on tin, originally used to decorate home altars."

stand out because their sounds are so distinct from those of English. This quality helps to remove the reader from his or her local environment and jar them into another world.

Beyond subjects like travel and culture, a non-English word can add a layer of meaning to any subject, as in this poem by Bill Kenney:

> *la petite mort* . . .
> as though I could
> live forever[4]

The French phrase is literally translated as "the little death," but, as many readers know, refers to an orgasm. The phrase is the linchpin of the poem: it sets the rhythm in place and confers a playfulness. If Kenney had instead used the English "orgasm," the poem would not be as lighthearted. Moreover, *la petite mort* adds an association that the English counterparts do not. The literal meaning of "mort" is death. Behind the light tone of the haiku stands an allusion to the cycle of sex, birth, and death.

English-language haiku can also accommodate words from languages with non-Latin scripts. However, inserting language with a different script or alphabet is risky as it can prove a disruptive experience. An English speaker can readily research

---

4. Bill Kenney, in *Modern Haiku* 42.3 (autumn 2011), 12.

a word in a language with a Latin-based alphabet. It's more difficult to do so for a word with a different character set. Languages that are written from right to left (Arabic and Hebrew, for instance) will require a layout that can accommodate bidirectional text. However, judiciously used, words from such languages can be useful, as in Lee Gurga's haiku:[5]

> Θάλαττα! θάλαττα!
> we patter around the deck
> in fair trade sandals
> ("*The sea! The sea!*" after *Xenophon*)

> slow motion rollers
> caress the glacial shore
> ᚳᛁᚷ ⁊ ᚢᛏᚠᚢᛋ
> ("*icy and eager*," from *Beowulf*)

Gurga borrows phrases from classical work in Ancient Greek and Old English[6] to throw relief upon our relationship with the sea. The first is a famous quote from *Anabasis*, when a retreating Greek army arrives to safety at the shore of the Black Sea. From *Beowulf*, the second quote is part of a description of the funeral of the king Shield Sheafson. In both poems, the immortality of the

---

5. Lee Gurga, in *Modern Haiku* 44.2 (summer 2013), 33.
6. Although a precursor to Modern English, Old English is sufficiently different so as to be considered a foreign language.

28

sea is contrasted with mortal humanity. In the first poem, the tone is humorous: the smallness of people and their concerns is represented by "patter" and "fair trade sandals." In the second, the tone is sober. The body of the deceased king is sent off in a ship to drift on the sea. The vessel that holds the king's body is characterized as "icy" (which indicates the season) and "eager." Despite the fact that the boat is laden with treasure and gear, the Beowulf narrator reflects that no one knows "who salvaged that load."[7] In each case, the Greek or Old English reinforces the distinction between us and the unknowable oceans. The non-Latin scripts make the words seem remote and impenetrable. The antiquity of the two languages also underscores the passing of time.

Although not using a Latin-based script, Japanese represents a special case for haiku poets.[8]

> after the ginko—
> still there, all the things
> I never noticed[9]

7. *Beowulf: A New Verse Translation*. Seamus Heaney, ed. (New York: Farrar, Straus and Giroux, 2000), 5. In the Heaney version, "icy and eager" is translated as "ice-clad, outbound" (5). I used "icy and eager" because of Gurga's reference.
8. A Latin-based script for Japanese does exist (rōmaji), which can make the language more accessible to Western readers. However, rōmaji is mainly used for non-Japanese speakers and learners.
9. Carlos Colón, in *Frogpond* 34:1 (Winter 2011), 30.

Most haiku poets know the meaning of the term *ginkō* (a haiku walk), and over time the word probably sheds some of its "foreign-ness" to our specialized community. But there is no direct counterpart in English. A word like "stroll" might be a usable ingredient, but it would not match the precise meaning that Carlos Colón intends. In contrast to a recreational stroll or walk, the *ginkō* is a practice with an explicit aim: to encourage the process of "noticing" and writing.

Over time many Japanese terms have migrated into English and become part of the language. They cover many aspects of life, including religion, the arts, cuisine, and sports.

> vintage kimono
> my seams unraveling
> this perfect life[10]

The use of "kimono" in this poem by Renée Owen raises a question: what defines a word as English? Where is the border between English and non-English words? As a word becomes prevalent in English usage, at what point does it become an English word? A formal solution would be to declare that a word has to be present in an authoritative resource (say, the *Oxford English Dictionary*) for it to

10. Renée Owen, in *Frogpond* 34:1 (Winter 2011), 30.

be accepted as English. But, of course, some words used in the United States are not used in the United Kingdom, not to mention other Anglophone countries.

For a writer, a strict ruling on a word may not be useful. A "borderline" word (one that retains an association with the original language but is becoming common in English) may be used effectively as a foreign word even if it's also recognized as an English one.

> slow down
> mañana still
> under construction[11]

"Mañana" is an example of a word that has made its way into English but is still closely associated with Spanish. The word's sounds are distinctly Spanish (for instance, the "eñe") and have not been Anglicized. This quality aids the word's centrality in the poem by Lauren Camp. In this poem, "mañana" acts like a Spanish, not an English, word.

This poem also shows one of the pitfalls of resorting to a foreign word. If "mañana" is replaced with "tomorrow," the tone and meaning change little. The word "mañana" is typically used in

11. Lauren Camp, in Matthew Chase-Daniel & Jerry Wellman, "Axle Contemporary's Haiku Roadsign Project" [photo-essay], *Frogpond* 35:1 (Winter 2012), 139.

informal slang and speech; it often implies slowing down. But this is not the overall tone of this haiku, and "tomorrow" seems as fitting a choice. In this case, the non-English word does not add much more value.

There can be significant benefits to using foreign words. A haiku is rooted in a specific time and place—and a foreign term or *kigo* can authentically reflect this. Similarly, a foreign language term may be better suited to a haiku or senryu with a cultural theme. Also, a non-English word may convey a sentiment or feeling that is distinct from its English counterpart. Finally, foreign vocabulary can add another layer of experience onto a haiku, and encourage readers to learn more beyond the poem.

Despite all of these benefits, the use of foreign terms also presents challenges. Non-English terms can be poor surrogates for English ones that are more concrete. Misused, the practice may be seen as a cliché or a device to salvage an otherwise unsuccessful poem. It's easy for foreign words to seem out of place and to be disruptive and confusing—distracting the reader from the whole poem.

As global travel and cross-border migrations continue to grow, and people of diverse cultures interact with greater frequency, it seems likely that the prevalence of multilingual vocabulary in haiku will only increase. Like any formal practice, the use of multilingual vocabulary offers opportunities and pitfalls to the poet. An awareness of these will help poets produce original and meaningful work.

WRITING HAIKU: THE TWO-LINE FORM

The majority of English-language haiku published today is, of course, written in a three-line format. One-liners have comprised a smaller (but increasing) share in recent years. But two-line haiku remain rare. For instance, in a recent issue of *Frogpond*, there were four two-line haiku and senryu out of a total of 197 poems. Similarly, a recent issue of *Modern Haiku* featured two out of 268. In *Take-Out Window*, the 2014 Haiku Society of America members' anthology, only four appeared in a collection of 291 poems.[1] These numbers prompt the question of why two-line haiku remain, in fact, "unicorns."[2]

Since the introduction of haiku into English the three-line form has predominated.[3] Much early scholarship defined haiku as a three-line poem.

---

1. *Frogpond* 38.1 (Winter 2015) and *Modern Haiku* 46.1 (Winter- Spring 2015). I tallied the poems in the "Haiku & Senryu" sections of each journal. *Take-Out Window: Haiku Society of America 2014 Members' Anthology*, Gary Hotham, ed. (New York: Haiku Society of America, 2014). In "Editor Comments," Hotham notes the paucity of submissions of two-liners (1).

2. My examination excludes two-liners that appear in linked forms like renku and rengay. In such cases, two-liners belong to a larger context and perform different or additional functions (e.g., stanza transitioning) than standalone two-line haiku.

3. There were exceptions. For example, Basil Hall Chamberlain translated into a two-line form. Refer to "Bashō and the Japanese Poetical Epigram" in *Transactions of the Asiatic Society of Japan*, Vol. XXX (Tokyo: Rikkyo Gakuin Press, 1902), 243–362. Google Books digital version. Accessed June 15, 2015.

Kenneth Yasuda wrote that haiku is a "one-breath poem in three lines."[4] James Hackett recommended that haiku poets "write in three lines . . ."[5] The early translations by Blyth, Henderson, and Yasuda were composed in this form. The Beat poets mainly wrote three-line haiku, which includes Jack Kerouac's popular work.

The weight of tradition is not the sole cause, however, for the persistence of three lines. Over the past century, English-language haiku poets have migrated from other established conventions, such as a strict seventeen-syllable count, for example. So what does account for the dearth of two-line haiku? While it seems unlikely that this format, which sits between the two preferred options, would be especially demanding, the two-liner does feature unique constraints. Simply put, the key qualities of English-language haiku are more difficult to achieve in a two-line structure.

A basic challenge of the two-line structure is rhythm, or meter. In English-language haiku, a short-long-short pattern predominates. This was true for the five-seven-five syllable count of early decades and for the more prevailing compact form today. Of course, a short-long-short pattern fits

4. Kenneth Yasuda, *A Pepper-Pod* (New York: Alfred A. Knopf, 1947), xv.
5. James Hackett, *Haiku Poetry: Original Verse in English, Volume One* (Tokyo: Japan Publications, Inc., 1968), 51.

organically into a haiku that is composed of three discrete units (lines). This is not the case with a two-line structure. Indeed, even when this pattern is present, it may not be as noticeable:

> after the quarrel . . .
> a singed peanut's lingering scent

The second line in this haiku by Jennifer Corpe[6] is fairly long, being composed of eight syllables. It does not feel unnatural to read the line with a pause between "a singed peanut's" and "lingering scent." This reading brings the poem closer to the three-unit standard.

Sometimes the sounds in a line are prolonged so that they prompt a slower-paced reading:

> first breath of spring
> **HarrrRRRRLEYS**

The onomatopoeic word "**HarrrRRRRLEYS**" accentuates the second line. Font size and letter case divide the line into two parts. Although not resulting in a strict short-long-short structure, the poem by Del Todey Turner[7] nevertheless feels longer overall than the total number of words (just five) would suggest.

6. Jennifer Corpe, *Frogpond* 34:1 (Winter 2011), 31.
7. Del Todey Turner, *Modern Haiku* 42.3 (Autumn 2011), 22.

Another common attribute of haiku, the pivot word or line, lends itself more to a three-line structure. Lee Gurga defines the pivot as "a word or phrase that combines with the forgoing text in one way and with the following text in another."[8] The second line often functions as (or contains) the pivot. In each of the haiku above, two images are present. In the first haiku, the images are "the quarrel" and "the singed peanut." In the second poem, the images are "first breath of spring" and Harleys. However, a pivot is absent in both of these. This is common in the two-line format, as also seen in this poem by David Reynolds:[9]

> same old argument
> rusty yo-yo

Due to space limitations, *kigo* and seasonal references are often treated differently, too. In a standard haiku, it is not unusual for a *kigo* to fully occupy one of the three lines. In a two-liner, this practice leaves the poem with only a single line for other material. This limitation can be addressed by using *kigo* that provide sufficient information:

8. Lee Gurga, *Haiku: A Poet's Guide* (Lincoln, IL: Modern Haiku Press, 2003), 78.
9. David C. Reynolds, *Modern Haiku* 45.2 (Summer 2014), 101.

october loneliness
two walking sticks

In Vincent Tripi's haiku,[10] the seasonal element "October loneliness"[11] conveys an experience of aging and disability. "Loneliness" underscores the association of autumn. If Tripi had omitted either word, readers would likely miss the full, rich meaning.

It's also helpful if the other line (without the *kigo*) is developed—suggestive enough—to shoulder the weight of conveying the experience:

a quiet kind of love
autumn crocus

In this haiku by Greg Piko,[12] "a quiet kind of love" points to the subject with "autumn crocus" as the *kigo*. A reader doesn't need additional context. But this approach carries a risk of saying too much or being heavy handed:

Slug trail on the porch . . .
now, I understand my life

---

10. Vincent Tripi in *The Haiku Anthology: Haiku and Senryu in English*, Cor van den Heuvel, ed. (New York: W. W. Norton & Company, 1999), 227.
11. The Yuki Teikei Haiku Season Word List. http://youngleaves.org/season-word-list/. Accessed August 9, 2015. The *kigo* listed is "autumn loneliness."
12. Greg Piko, *Modern Haiku* 42.3 (Autumn 2011), 76.

In David Rosen's haiku,[13] the image of the "slug trail" anticipates the insight expressed in line two. However, the second line verges toward being too declarative (for a haiku). Rosen explicitly connects the image to the meaning for the reader.

The experience of cutting and the usage of a *kireji* (a cutting word) are different in a two-liner. Punctuation like ellipses and dashes, which can be substitutes for *kireji* in English, are used (as in Rosen's haiku earlier). But there are other techniques—for instance, extra spacing—that are economical in a compact space:

> Deep in the smell of childhood
> comic books winter rain

In this poem by Scott Terrill,[14] an extra space is inserted between the words "in" and "the" in line one, and "books" and "winter" in line two. If these additional spaces were not present, there would only be one option for the cut: the end of the first line. The spacing has produced two new potential cut points that compel the reader to pause. This results in a rhythm that feels unique when compared to many other haiku.

---

13. David Rosen. "Your Daily Poem" website. http://www.yourdailypoem. com/listpoem.jsp?poem_id=1848. Accessed June 6, 2015.

14. Scott Terrill in *Fear of Dancing: The Red Moon Anthology of English-Language Haiku* 2013 (Winchester, VA: Red Moon Press, 2014), 74.

Another hallmark of haiku is its open-ended character. When Eric Amman considered the two-line form, he argued that "the two lines balance each other, tending to 'close' the poem."[15] While this assessment may be too categorical, it is true that an additional (third) line, especially when employing a *kigo* or a seasonal reference, can create a sense of space and also accommodate a shift between two parts. Jim Kacian observes: "One or three lines has offered a more flexible handling of material without losing the music, asymmetry, surprise . . ."[16]

Beyond this range of haiku-specific challenges, another notable constraint of the two-line poem is that it leaves the poet with less material to develop. By reducing the number of lines to two, the poet surrenders one-third of the units to work with. This limits the opportunity for lineation (enjambment and end-stopping).

The differences inherent in the two-line haiku add up: varying rhythms, restrained pivoting and cutting, less room for a seasonal element, and less opportunity for lineation. When combining these factors, it's apparent that the two-line form is unique and sometimes unforgiving. Even if a two-liner is successful in working with these constraints,

---

15. Eric W. Amman, *The Wordless Poem: A Study of Zen in Haiku* (*Haiku Magazine* – Special Issue, Vol. III, No. V), 37.
16. Jim Kacian, "Identifying UFOs," *Modern Haiku* 45.2 (Summer 2014), 48.

that success may still feel very different from the haiku that readers are familiar with and expect.

Considering these handicaps, why resort to the two-line haiku? What benefits does this structure offer? There are, in fact, several qualities that make it a useful option. The first of these can be termed "proximity." As illustrated above, the absence of a pivot or another transitional element has the effect of joining two images. There is a risk of tying the images too tightly, and losing the shift between them. However, if well executed, the result can be a potent concentration of images:

> deserted tennis court
> wind through the net

In this haiku by Gary Hotham,[17] the two images are presented sequentially and with no mediating element. Each conveys emptiness and loneliness. The first image does so of its own accord (through the use of the word "deserted"). With this context set, the second image adds to the feeling.

By leaving out more concrete description than the three-line format, the reliance on suggestion

---

17. Gary Hotham in *Haiku in English: The First Hundred Years*, Jim Kacian, Philip Rowland, and Allan Burns, eds. (New York: W. W. Norton & Company, 2013), 40.

may be even stronger. In this poem by Karen Sohne,[18] the background is wholly absent:

> androgynous stranger
> winks at me

An additional line might provide detail such as a setting or a season. As it stands, the reader is left with only a snapshot of an interaction, and nothing more.

Two-line haiku also afford the opportunity to compose longer lines, as in this poem by Robert Boldman:[19]

> Death camp in the photograph
> the little girl's hair will always be blowing

The first line contains seven syllables and the second contains eleven syllables, for a total of eighteen. In these terms, this poem is longer than is customary in haiku today (whether in two or three lines). The second line is able to accommodate an adjective ("little") and the present participle "will always be blowing" (rather than the present tense "blows" or "blowing"). A two-liner can afford the

18. Karen Sohne in *The Haiku Anthology: Haiku and Senryu in English*, Cor van den Heuvel, ed. (New York: W. W. Norton & Company, 1999), 187.
19. Robert Boldman in *Haiku in English: The First Hundred Years*, Kacian, Rowland, and Burns, eds., 87.

poet an opportunity to experiment with longer lines while conforming to the traditional overall word volume.

The opposite is true as well. Two-line haiku can approximate the shorter feel of the one-liner. Jörgen Johansson's poem is an example:[20]

> a ladybird
> b5 to c4

In this haiku, the two images are presented with no intervening component. Because it is composed in two lines, the reader pauses at the end of the first line. However, it's easy to imagine this poem as a one-liner: "a ladybird b5 to c4." The result is a quicker read but not radically different from the original.

English-language haiku has grown more diverse over time. It remains to be seen if two-line haiku become more common or remain sparse. If poets do produce more two-liners, they may discover new strengths of the form and overcome some of its constraints. As it stands, haiku poets will benefit if they consider the two-line format as a viable option when composing their work.

---

20. Jörgen Johansson, in *Haiku in English: The First Hundred Years*, Kacian, Rowland, and Burns, eds., 252.

The Twin Pleasures of *Kigo*

In haiku the kigo often plays the role of a supporting actor. The Haiku Society of America defines kigo as "a word or phrase that helps identify the season of the experience recorded in the poem."[1] While the kigo is not *the* central experience, its function is instrumental as an aid for the reader to access that experience.

In some haiku, however, the kigo moves beyond this secondary role and shares the spotlight:

> eucalyptus grove—
> the painting teacher
> adds blue to the green[2]

For example in this haiku, by the poet with the pseudonym "ash of moth," the kigo is used to convey an experience of learning and teaching. The poem also calls attention to the eucalyptus grove. Upon reading, my mind jumped to an image of the tree (common in California) and the hue of its sickle-shaped leaves. I found myself examining

---

1. Haiku Society of America website. "Official Definitions of Haiku and Related Terms." http://hsa-haiku.org/archives/HSA_Definitions_2004. html#Haiku. Accessed January 25, 2014.

2. aom (tim). Shiki Monthly Kukai - November 2011. https:// sites.google. com/site/shikikukaitemporaryarchives/home/november-2011-kukai. Accessed January 25, 2014.

a eucalyptus on a subsequent walk. Through the kigo this haiku offers reflections about teaching *and* about the eucalyptus itself.

> firesky ridge—
> the tanager drinks
> his own red[3]

Allan Burns' haiku paints a picture of a tanager with a "firesky" backdrop. A reader with no knowledge about tanagers will instantly grasp that at least some tanagers posses red in their coats. Burns educates the reader about the bird (or reminds those who already know). He evokes an important characteristic of the creature.

Although the kigo plays a critical support function, it is also an important element in its own right. A kigo is typically used to provide seasonal context and help the reader participate in the moment. But in some haiku the kigo—whether a bird or flower, or the sun or rain—also conveys insights about the world in which we live.

---

3. Allan Burns, *Acorn* (No. 31: Fall 2013), 60.

LEAPING HAIKU

At the April 2003 HPNC meeting, Paul Miller presented a paper on the element of surprise in haiku. He posited that haiku can be divided into several types, one of which he termed "non-intellectualized" haiku.[1] This type of haiku could also be described as intuitive, associative, or non-literal.

Robert Bly describes the intuitive approach to poetry as "leaping" because leaps are taken "from the conscious to the unconscious and back again."[2] Leaping, associative poetry is tricky to achieve because subconscious images may not be accessible to a reader.

I'd like to examine two poems, one with a logical leap that stays in the conscious realm and one with an intuitive leap that dips into the subconscious. The first is a senryu by Carolyne Rohrig:

> still jobless
> another orange peel
> on the compost heap[3]

---

1. Paul Miller, unpublished paper.
2. Robert Bly (editor). *Leaping Poetry: An Idea with Poems and Translations.* Boston: Beacon Press, 1972: p. 1.
3. Carolyne Rohrig, *Mariposa* 7.

The poem opens with the context—"still jobless." The poem then leaps to the image of "another orange peel / on the compost heap." This image underscores the experience of joblessness by highlighting one characteristic of it, ennui.

The key point to note is that this image does its work in the conscious, literal realm. The reader is able to visualize the orange peel on the compost heap, and can make a rational connection between this image and the intent of the poem—to convey an experience of joblessness.

Like Rohrig's, the following senryu by Laurie Stoelting also presents strong imagery:

> my propped pillow
> our vacation
> starts to rain[4]

In contrast, Stoelting's images are deployed in a non-rational way. While it can certainly rain during a vacation, a vacation itself, of course, can't literally "start to rain." Also, what does the "propped pillow" have to do with it? This poem nicely compels the reader to make an imaginative leap and feel his or her way to a meaning.

4. Laurie Stoelting, *Mariposa* 7.

Both literal and non-literal poetry are rewarding, but in different ways. It's easier to misunderstand or undervalue non-literal poetry because of the comprehension barrier. This is unfortunate, because the reader is rewarded with the understanding that comes from making this kind of leap.

HAIKU AND SENRYU

spring cleaning—
moving the dust
from one season to another

I blink and the fox disappears—
scent of wildflower

first warm day
the ringing bells
of the paletas cart

Trevi fountain
two lovers
quarrel over a map

we speak to each other
with travelers' gestures
three-quarter moon

mixing red and yellow paint
my son discovers
fire

all the boys
stop to watch the train—
spring wind

Bar Mitzvah
on top of his Mohawk
a yarmulke

spring dusk—
catching the last
fly ball

coat still glossy
the dead crow—
changing season

BEYOND THE TRAILHEAD:
LAURIE STOELTING'S HAIKU

Sometimes, the best haiku is local. Bashō noted that "a haiku is simply what is happening in this particular place and at this particular time."[1] Haiku poets often produce memorable work when writing about the places they know most intimately.

Laurie Stoelting's work exemplifies this. For many years, Stoelting lived in the town of Mill Valley (California), near the wilderness areas of Mt. Tamalpais, Muir Woods, and Point Reyes. The ecosystems of these Northern California locales pervade her poetry.

again, the finch's warble
these woods are rich
with purple iris[2]

Throughout Stoelting's work, there is unflagging attention to detail—to the flora and fauna of her neighborhood. Sound, color, smell, and even temperature are absorbed.

---

1. Eric W. Amman, *The Wordless Poem: A Study of Zen in Haiku* (*Haiku Magazine*—Special Issue, Vol. III, No. V), 20.
2. Laurie W. Stoelting, *Light on the Mountain: Mt. Tamalpais, A Poet's View* (Field Trips, 2000 & 2009), 17.

out of the gully bird call
hot scent
of chaparral[3]

Much of Stoelting's work follows the classic *shasei* tradition of nature sketches. Indeed, in some of her haiku, no person is present.

the single rivulet
how slowly a pond
lets go[4]

to a chorus of crickets
the earth
gives up its light[5]

In each of these poems, the focus is exclusively on the natural elements: the pond and the crickets. Of course, these are not purely descriptive. In the first haiku, Stoelting has imbued the pond with a quality of not "letting go." However, this is not a personification of the pond, but rather an observation of a natural process, a pond releasing itself.

In the second poem, the word "light" is literal, referring to the transition from light to darkness

---

3. Ibid., 38.
4. Ibid., 41.
5. Ibid., 45.

that dusk brings. But the light also denotes the relationship of the crickets and their habitat. Stoelting doesn't highlight the unity of people and crickets, nor of people and earth, but rather of crickets and earth. What this haiku portrays is not people-centric. To borrow Eric Amman's language, it is not "anthropo-centered" as it portrays a world "outside the poet, outside man, outside the limited human frame of reference."[6] For Stoelting, this doesn't trigger a feeling of unimportance or of being peripheral. Indeed, she celebrates it.

When a person is present in Stoelting's haiku, she or he typically acts as a receiver: gaining access to the gifts that nature bestows. The gift may simply be an appreciation of the beauty of an ordinary thing.

> the hummingbird's red throat
> he stops
> my breath[7]

Of course, those who receive the gifts are those who are prepared, possessing attentiveness and an open mind.

---

6. Eric W. Amman, *The Wordless Poem: A Study of Zen in Haiku* (*Haiku Magazine*—Special Issue, Vol. III, No. V), 11.
7. Laurie W. Stoelting, *Light on the Mountain: Mt. Tamalpais, A Poet's View* (Field Trips, 2000 & 2009), 30.

high meadow
   opening myself
to the mountain's face[8]

In this haiku, the speaker is actively seeking communion with the mountain. This communion may be an experience of the mountain as a calming influence or as a space for reflection. Or, it may be a spiritual or religious event. Whatever the case, the poet encourages us to rely upon nature as a refuge from life's daily labors:

highway's surge—
I walk deeper
into the steep ravine[9]

Of course, impatience may subvert the opportunity for any of these experiences. So too may youth or inexperience.

yanking out dandelions—
when I was young
we blew their heads off[10]

Stoelting portrays herself in this poem as a child that opted for the instant gratification of blowing

8. Ibid., 14.
9. Ibid., 2.
10. Laurie Stoelting, *Mariposa*, Issue 8 (Spring/Summer 2003), 13.

apart the dandelions. The word "yanking" feels abrupt, and reflection on this provokes a tinge of sadness and loss.

Following the trail of Stoelting's poems, we can infer a cluster of ideas centered around nature. One major idea is the unity of all creation. To our senses, the things of this world seem discrete and separate. But if we more closely examine our surroundings, we can grasp an underlying interconnectedness.

> out of the hermit thrush
> out of the valley
> one song[11]

This understanding is probably one reason why the non-anthropocentric reality does not cause anxiety. The poet has a stake in all things and in uncovering their relationships.

A second theme is the idea of epiphany through contact with nature. As described above, in Stoelting's work the experience of epiphany is broadly interpreted, and is not strictly religious.

Of course, these two ideas are not new. In the hands of a less mature writer, this might only have produced repetition of well-worn themes — derivative work. What makes Stoelting's

---

11. Laurie W. Stoelting, *Light on the Mountain: Mt. Tamalpais, A Poet's View* (Field Trips, 2000 & 2009), 13.

haiku so compelling is that her haiku approach these not as intellectual ideas, but rather as experiences. Stoelting wrote, "I had the habit of writing as I walked Mt. Tamalpais. The poems started with feelings, awareness . . . when I was introduced to haiku awareness found words."[12] Direct experience helped Stoelting to compose lasting work.

Stoelting's haiku are rewarding for many reasons: strong descriptions, supple language, a receptive voice, and a durable linkage of nature with human concerns. But what makes them more special is what the title of her book *Light on the Mountain* suggests. For those who want it, there is something to be gained beyond the trailhead. Laurie's poems can show you the path.

12. Ibid., no page number.

The Trickster: An Introduction to Patrick Gallagher's Haiku

Patrick Gallagher has been writing haiku for over a decade, and has been active in two historic haiku groups in California—the Yuki Teikei Haiku Society and the Haiku Poets of Northern California. Readers familiar with Gallagher's haiku and senryu know that an offbeat sensibility and a lively sense of humor are hallmarks of his poetry. I'd like to examine the use of humor in Gallagher's poetry, and introduce his distinctive voice to readers who may not be familiar with him.

Like the trickster figure of mythology, humor appears in a variety of guises in Gallagher's poetry. Many of Gallagher's senryu are exuberant and even a bit zany.

> the buzz!
> this must be a very important
> fly[1]

In this senryu, a key word—"buzz"—jumps out at the reader. "Buzz" is a colloquial, onomatopoetic word that shows the poet is unafraid to appear less than decorous. Larger concepts are filtered through the playfulness, of course. The senryu

---

1. *Mariposa* 5, Fall/Winter 2001: 15.

mocks the seemingly inconsequential fly, and in so doing implicitly acknowledges the fly's (and poet's) essential place in the world.

> warm water spray
> from the heated toilet seat
> modern Japan yah[2]

In this poem, the word "yah" functions as an exclamation point. Like "buzz," "yah" is an informal word that gives the poem a playful feel. This senryu illustrates the layers of tradition and modernity in Japan—and how an even well informed Westerner might react to this dynamic.

In both poems, Gallagher's humor revolves around—and is partly rooted in—a single, unconventional word. These words also provide the added benefit of making the poem more present. That is, they draw the reader in so that he or she feels that they are actually in the scene.[3]

At the other pole, Gallagher employs a more sober humor, too. In many of his poems, the humor is bittersweet.

2. owen, w. f. (ed). *If I Met Basho*. San Francisco: Two Autumns Press, 2005: 8. Note: This haiku originally appeared within a haibun; see *Contemporary Haibun Online*, Vol. 1 - http://www.poetrylives.com/CHO/ahhv1/Gallagher.html.
3. This use of non-conventional words also occurs in Gallagher's non-humorous poetry. For example: summer night / the cha!-ch-ch, cha!-ch-ch / of switch engines (Higginson, William. *Haiku World: An International Poetry Almanac*. Tokyo: Kodansha International, 1996: 107.)

a bench in shade
the old couple plotting
their next moves[4]

quiet moon
the bachelor boys
moved away[5]

The first senryu quietly laments the pains of growing old. The second poem mourns not only the departure of the lively, young neighbors but also the loss of bachelorhood itself. Each is wistful, and exemplifies the comedian Carol Burnett's well-known observation that "comedy is tragedy plus time."[6] While these two poems don't hinge on a single word, they nevertheless exhibit skillful word choice. For example, the words "plotting" in the first poem and "moon" in the second are older words with Anglo-Saxon roots. Typical of such words, they are visceral and vivid.[7] Also, although more subdued, each poem hovers on the edge of the exuberance evident in the other poems. If the poems were a little longer, the reader could easily imagine that the restraint would fall away and zaniness would burst out.

4. owen, w. f. (ed). *If I Met Basho*. San Francisco: Two Autumns Press, 2005: 8.
5. *Raw Nervz*, Vol. II, No. 3 (Fall 2001): 30.
6. *Wikipedia* - Wikiquote: http://en.wikiquote.org/wiki/Carol_Burnett.
7. Gardner, John. *The Art of Fiction: Notes on Craft for Young Writers*. New York: Vintage Books, 1991: 98.

This contagious exuberance is a hallmark of Gallagher's poetry. Whether bittersweet or just downright funny, Gallagher's poetry is full of surprise.

J. D. Salinger and Haiku

J. D. Salinger is best known as the author of *The Catcher in the Rye*, the controversial novel of teenage angst. Salinger is also famous for his reclusiveness: he has not published in forty years and fiercely guards his privacy. For haiku writers, there's another, equally intriguing Salinger: haiku devotee. Haiku figure prominently in Salinger's stories about the fictional Glass family, and it is clear that Salinger studied, and was strongly attracted to, haiku.

I.

The Catcher in the Rye was Salinger's first novel and vaulted him to fame in 1951. However, the majority of Salinger's published work focuses on the fictional Glass family. This eccentric family is comprised of two parents—retired vaudeville performers—and their seven precocious children, each of whom starred at different times on a children's radio quiz show from the nineteen-twenties to the nineteen-forties.

Salinger published two books and several short stories about the Glass family. Published in 1961, *Franny and Zooey* focuses on the two youngest siblings. In 1963, Salinger published a book comprised of two stories: *Raise High the Roof Beam, Carpenters* and *Seymour: An Introduction*. The former relates the story of the eldest child's (Seymour) wedding day, and the latter is a reminiscence of Seymour by the second eldest sibling, Buddy. The collection *Nine Stories* contains three Glass family short stories.

While the stories involve different members of the family, a principal subject of all of the stories is Seymour. Seymour was the driving force behind many of the younger siblings. Seymour became the family's central trauma when he committed suicide at the age of thirty-one, haunted by his experiences as a soldier in World War II. Coping with this event is a central theme elaborated in all of the stories.

II.

Seymour became interested in Buddhism and Hinduism, and Eastern poetry, at an early age. In *Seymour: An Introduction*, Buddy writes, "During much of his adolescence, and all his adult life, Seymour was drawn, first, to Chinese poetry, and then, as deeply, to Japanese poetry, and to both in ways that he was drawn to no other poetry in the world."[1] According to Buddy, Seymour's greatest

1. J. D. Salinger, *Raise High the Roof Beam, Carpenters* and *Seymour: An Introduction* (New York: Bantam Books, 1981), 117.

passion was haiku: "Seymour probably loved the classical Japanese three-line, seventeen-syllable haiku as he loved no other form of poetry, and . . . he himself wrote — bled — haiku."[2]

In fact, even when Seymour wasn't writing haiku, his poetry was still influenced by the form. Buddy describes Seymour's later poetry as "substantially like an English translation of a sort of double haiku . . . a six-line verse, of no certain accent but usually more iambic than not . . . deliberately held down to thirty-four syllables, or twice the number of the classical haiku."[3] These poems were "as bare as possible, and invariably ungarnished."[4]

The reader sees Seymour's attachment to haiku in other ways, too. For instance, Seymour wrote in his diary that when he and his fiancé debated the merits of a movie, he quoted R. H. Blyth's definition of sentimentality to bolster his point: "we are being sentimental when we give to a thing more tenderness than God gives to it."[5] Later in the same passage, Seymour turns to the poet Saigyo to describe the tenderness he feels towards his fiancé: "What it is I know not / But with the gratitude / my tears fall."[6]

---

2. Ibid, 126-7.
3. Ibid, 127.
4. Ibid, 129.
5. Ibid, 67.
6. Ibid, 67-8.

Buddy, too, has been deeply influenced by haiku. He says that haiku can enlighten and impact him "to within an inch of his life."[7] While explaining Seymour's interest in haiku in *Seymour: An Introduction*, Buddy digresses from the narrative and launches into a discussion of the merits of haiku, inviting the reader to learn more about Chinese poetry and haiku. He even comments upon the quality of available English translations. He declares: "If, in the line of duty, I should incidentally titillate a few young people's interest in Chinese and Japanese poetry, it would be very good news to me."[8]

Besides the prominence of haiku in his characters' lives, the importance of haiku to Salinger can be seen in another way: its pivotal role in plot and theme. Buddy writes that when he arrived at the hotel room where Seymour committed suicide, he found a haiku that Seymour wrote that day: "The little girl on the plane / Who turned her doll's head around / To look at me."[9]

That a haiku occupies such a key place in the story is instructive. It's a symbol of its importance

---

7. Ibid, 118.
8. Ibid.
9. J. D. Salinger, *Franny and Zooey* (New York: Bantam Books, 1985), 64. I have quoted the poem exactly as it appears in the book. This format does not show whether Salinger intended all three lines to be flush left, or arranged in a different way.

to Seymour—and to Salinger, who relies on it to say something about his character.

The same is true in another story, this one not about the Glass family. In the story "Teddy," the main character is a ten-year old, religious-mystical prodigy of sorts. He is thought to be able to predict the future, and is being studied by academics. Shortly before the climax, Teddy quotes two haiku by Bashō:

"'Nothing in the voice of the cicada intimates how soon it will die,'" Teddy said suddenly. "'Along this road goes no one, this autumn eve.'"[10]

These poems foreshadow the climax of the story, and offer a possible explanation of Teddy's motives.

In summary, in Salinger's stories, haiku are important to the main characters and also play a key role in the story line. That is, Salinger uses haiku not only to add texture to his characters, but also to provide keys to his stories' plots and themes.

III.

Salinger was clearly well read on the subject of haiku and was deeply attracted to the form. However, the details of his interest in haiku remain a mystery—much like other facets of his life.

---

10. J. D. Salinger, *Nine Stories* (Boston: Little, Brown and Company, 1991), 185.

It is known that Salinger was interested in Zen Buddhism for many years, and his love of haiku was probably related to this. But the exact relationship is impossible to ascertain.

So, too, is an even more intriguing possibility: Salinger writing haiku.[11] Was the haiku by his character Seymour the only one Salinger wrote, or are there others? Is Salinger, today, still interested in haiku? Is he writing any? Like other mysteries of J. D. Salinger, the answer will have to wait.

---

11. It's notable that none of the haiku used in the stories (all quoted above) follow the five-seven-five syllable format. Even though Buddy describes haiku as a three-line, seventeen syllable form, it's unknown what Salinger's opinions were on this matter.

THE HALF-FINISHED BRIDGE: INTRODUCTION

> First snow
> falling
> on the half-finished bridge.
> —Bashō (translated by Robert Hass)

We can never predict the events of our lives, as the bridge builders in Bashō's haiku can attest.[1] The four poets featured in this year's Two Autumns, the twenty-fifth in the longstanding series, have each built a significant body of work over time. I anticipate that each possesses an equally long or greater road ahead of haiku writing. When a "first snow" arrives, each of these poets will possess a reservoir from which to draw new work.

Rich Krivcher's poetry is well known for humor and a sometimes offbeat sensibility. His funny senryu have garnered awards in contests over many years. Indeed, I have laughed long (and out loud) at many of his poems.

> condoms:
> the checker asks me to slide
> my card more slowly

---

1. Bashō. In *The Essential Haiku: Versions of Bashō, Buson, and Issa*, ed. and trans. Robert Hass. Hopewell, NJ: The Ecco Press, 1994, p. 32.

Krivcher's humor runs in many shades, from the up-front and hilarious to the understated and subtle. Krivcher notes, "My mind tends more toward senryu than haiku, especially at this stage of my life." Despite this, it would be a mistake to neglect his sober toned poems.

> word of his death . . .
> the long walk
> from the mailbox

This poem is a quintessential haiku, focusing with clarity on a single moment. He perfectly captures the initial shock and sadness that we feel upon hearing of the unexpected passing of a loved one. As befits a poet with a long career, Krivcher's work is multidimensional.

Tanya McDonald's haiku also cover a variety of topics and range over wide emotional terrain. One thread that runs through her work is an engagement with social and political issues. This is no easy task in haiku. The brevity of the form tempts a less experienced poet into an unnuanced sound-bite—the opposite of a good haiku.

> nature talk—
> she erases "native peoples"
> from the chalkboard

In this poem, McDonald employs a light touch, simply describing a small act in a classroom. In so doing, she evokes the sweep of the history of indigenous peoples in North America. But she leaves the subject open ended, trusting the reader to consider the implications.

B-2 flyover
for a moment I forget
its purpose

The same applies in this poem. McDonald does not fall into the trap of casual judgment. The B-2 "Stealth" bomber is, from an aesthetic perspective, a sleek and gorgeous object. But of course it is designed to unleash destruction. McDonald notes the contradiction, but again leaves the poem in the reader's hands. This is the mark of a patient and mature approach.

Linda Papanicolaou is recognized not only as a haiku poet but also as a haiga artist. Images are key to making a haiku compelling and lasting. Such imagery is a hallmark of Papanicolaou's work.

the sweetness
of the canyon shade —
blue-eyed Mary

Color is a notable ingredient in many of her haiku, as shown in "blue-eyed Mary." Papanicolaou uses other visual cues as well. Concrete and descriptive language about everyday things, and about the natural world, populate her haiku.

> stadium lights
> through the mask of a helmet
> the face of a child

In three lines, and with a single image, Papanicolaou's poem prompts reflection upon American youth sports culture and the toll it can exert on our young.

As a young man, Joseph Robello served in the Coast Guard. His poems often reference the sailor's life and this experience connects his work to many writers before him.

> back splicing
> a mooring line
> talk of home

Tangible images of the sea life pervade his work and grant Robello a unique voice in today's haiku landscape. A strong helping of Zen runs through Robello's haiku as well.

humming
the length of the walk home
plum blossoms

Blyth noted that the Zen concept of "loneliness" is "not that of the poet as a recluse." Rather, it is "above all in a nameless realm where the human and the non-human . . . meet and are one."[2] It is a refined experience, one that Robello expresses well.

The work of these four haiku poets is even more diverse than what is displayed in these pages, which inevitably reflects the tastes and interests of the editor. My hope is that this taste will lead you to explore more from this fine quartet.

2. R. H. Blyth. *Haiku: Eastern Culture* (*Volume I*). Japan: Hokuseido, 1964, p. 177.

> I go
> you stay;
> two autumns

Much has been written about Shiki's famous haiku, the namesake of this reading series, now in its nineteenth year. A central element in the poem is the implied idea of the individual journey. In the poem, two people take leave of one another; each is on a separate, personal journey.

Of course, each of us is on a journey— simply by virtue of being alive. One delight of reading haiku is identifying with the common experiences that life brings. We are all fellow travelers on the road of life, experiencing love, loss, growth, and fulfillment. The only constant is change, "moonlight changing direction," as Christopher Herold notes.

The four distinguished poets assembled here—Fay Aoyagi, Christopher Herold, John Stevenson, and Billie Wilson—all came to haiku from different backgrounds. Each possesses a unique approach to the haiku tradition, and each takes the reader along a distinctive path.

long night
I distort the globe
with Photoshop

Fay Aoyagi notes, "I don't write haiku to report the weather. I write to tell my stories." Great stories often result from tension. Fay's haiku transverse multiple worlds: Japan and America, the Japanese and English languages, immigrant and native experiences, modernity and tradition, male and female. The interplay of (and tensions between) these multiple poles produces haiku of stunning clarity.

Pearl Harbor Day
a perfect ship
in the glass bottle

This poem threads together and crystallizes the touchpoints of several worlds. It also neatly ties in personal and national histories.

Fay notes that she does not write traditional haiku, preferring to stray off Bashō's path. Because of her experimental approach, Fay's haiku retain an element of mystery, an essential ingredient of much great poetry. Her poetry is not always literal; she requires the reader to take imaginative leaps:

through a keyhole
I watch the summer
of my childhood

Christopher Herold remembers that as a young man he would sit still and absorb the sights and sounds of the world around him, which led him to later practice meditation. This quiet, open, and receptive approach enables Christopher to notice the smallest happenings, an essential skill for the haiku poet.

a slight breeze
all the colors telegraph
along the spider's line

This quality of alertness seeps through Christopher's haiku, where the reader can almost "feel the quiet":

early twilight
snow enters the barn
on the backs of cows

Quiet, in this sense, is not literal silence. It is a "way" that allows Christopher to hear more. For example, a professional musician, he is adept at calling attention to sounds that readers may overlook.

downpour
the one sound of so many
surfaces

In contrast to Christopher, the approach that
John Stevenson takes is more akin to that of an
actor, which he has been for over twenty years.
There is tension, drama, and flair in John's poetry.

Colonel Mustard
in the library . . .
winter night

An accomplished actor knows that great work
results from taking chances. For instance, taking
the risk of appearing silly or undignified can be
an obstacle that some artists (of any genre) never
surmount. John's haiku is more compelling for it.
As with the other writers here, John is a careful
observer of human activity, waiting for the right
opportunity to present itself.

a change in their voices
children finding
a fledging

From funny to sober to mystical, John's voice is capable of great range, and his poetry delights and engages through many readings.

> fireworks
> I close my eyes
> for a second look

Close experience with, and observation of, nature is the centerpiece of the haiku tradition. Residing in Alaska for more than four decades, Billie Wilson's haiku is deeply about place.

> flattened grass
> where the bear slept
> stink of salmon

Billie's poetry is successful because she uses all of the senses to evoke place. She gives the reader a visceral experience of a place, as she does with the above poem, which employs strong and distinct visual, tactile, and aural elements.

Like the other poets here, Billie's poetry also retains the capacity to surprise.

leaves turned gold—
he still knows all the words
to that old love song

Billie's poetry, like much classic haiku, has a strong foundation in nature. Ultimately, she reminds us why the physical world around us is so important—to her, and to us.

choosing a melon—
a song so old
I forget why I cry

The poets gathered in this volume offer four very different strands of the haiku tradition—past and present. Each has retained a distinct voice and set of concerns.

Though different in their particulars, the work of these four poets mirrors the same journey that we all take. The haiku and senryu of Fay, Christopher, John, and Billie engage, delight, teach, and console. For these gifts, we owe our gratitude.

Haiku and Senryu

midday heat—
the stoplight turns
more slowly

day laborers
hunch on the corner—
summer haze

water—
clear enough
to hide all secrets

summer afternoon the sun filling with Shabbat

dawn—
the weight
of the coming rain

teapot
  whistles
I mark the page

Two men shaking hands
      —one man
for the moment

two beer bottles
left on the front steps—
summer evening

crack of the bat
quieter at dusk—
Father's Day

first day of school
his backpack
filled with summer

THE "ANCIENT ENEMY": DEATH IN ART AND HAIKU

When to the moment I shall say,
"Linger awhile! So fair thou art!"
Goethe, *The Tragedy of Faust—Part I*[1]

In 1964 Andy Warhol began enlisting visitors to his studio for what would become his famous "screen tests."[2] Over a three-year period, Warhol and his crew posed nearly five hundred visitors for three-minute film portraits. Subjects ranged from friends to famous artists to street hustlers. These portraits were impromptu, unscripted, filmed in black and white, and shot in close-up. Sometimes Warhol would turn on the camera and leave the subject alone for the duration of the portrait. The subjects usually engaged in minor dramatic action such as making faces, smoking, or holding a pose.

The portraits are important from a critical perspective for many reasons—as an example of Warhol's approach to pictorial composition, for

1. Johann Wolfgang von Goethe. *The Tragedy of Faust—Part I*. Translated by Anna Swanwick. New York: P. F. Collier & Son, 1909–14. Online edition: <http://www.bartleby.com/19/1/>. Stephen Koch quotes this passage in Ric Burns, *Andy Warhol: A Documentary Film*. <http://www.pbs.org/wnet/americanmasters/database/warhol_a.html>.

2. Callie Angell. *Andy Warhol Screen Tests: The Films of Andy Warhol Catalogue Raisonné, Volume 1*. New York: Abrams and the Whitney Museum of American Art, 2006, 12.

instance.[3] For haiku writers there is another reason why they are so compelling.

The most startling aspect of the portraits may be seeing the subjects—from the famous to the unknown alike—as they no longer are. Watching the films, we recognize that these people we are viewing no longer exist as they do on the screen. They have aged by over four decades; some have passed away. The qualities of youth, so evident on screen, have vanished—victims of "the murderous passage of time."[4]

> Old photographs:
> how I long to know my parents
> before I was born.[5]

Though best known by the general public as the doyen of Pop Art, Warhol's preoccupation throughout his career was what the film portraits reveal—the tenuousness of time, the brevity of life, and, finally, death.[6] The critic Stephen Koch notes: "His genius was for immediacy and for an absolute refusal to tell a story. Just: this is it, this is it. Nothing <u>more: nothing</u> before, nothing after. Not where

3. Stephen Koch, *Stargazer: The Life, World and Films of Andy Warhol*. New York & London: Marion Boyars, 1991, 56.
4. Ibid., 12.
5. James Luguri, in Jerry Ball, Garry Gay, and Tom Tico, editors. *The San Francisco Haiku Anthology*. Windsor, Calif.: Smythe-Waithe Press, 1992, 156.
6. Koch, *Stargazer*, 133.

we're going, not where we've been. Just right now. I think he was an artist dealing with immediacy, intensity, vividness, power of connection—and the threat to all of that that comes with death."[7]

twilight deepens
the wordless things
I know[8]

As Warhol understood, focusing on the moment—by its very definition—implies a brush with death. This is because we are always losing the moment; as soon as we notice or appreciate the present moment it is gone. Our mortality is thus revealed in the ever-changing instants of daily life.

Haiku poets, too, uncover the fleetingness of time by focusing on the moment. Francine Porad's haiku, quoted above, refers to twilight, known as an epitome of transience and impermanence: the death of day and the birth of night.

on the patio
the afternoon drifts along
with the butterfly[9]

7. Koch quoted from Burns, *Andy Warhol.*
8. Francine Porad, in Bruce Ross. *How to Haiku: A Writer's Guide to Haiku and Related Forms.* Boston: Charles E. Tuttle Co., 2002, 16.
9. Patricia Machmiller, in Ball, et al. *The San Francisco Haiku Anthology,* 10.

In this poem the afternoon "drifts along" but is still short-lived, as Patricia Machmiller reminds us. Our experience is often that all summer afternoons are too fleeting. For that matter, summer itself passes too quickly. Before you know it, many summers have come and gone.

old garden shed
the insecticide can
full of spiders[10]

As the above poems show, haiku poets cope with the fickleness of time in the seasons and the natural world. Our very attention to the natural world implies recognition of change— death and rebirth. However, it comes as no surprise that we confront change and the prospect of death most directly in our bodies and our relationships.

year of the monkey—
the hair in my ears
grows thicker[11]

As Jerry Kilbride noted, we experience change in

10. Ernest Berry, in Jim Kacian and the Red Moon editorial staff, editors. *A Glimpse of Red: The Red Moon Anthology of English-Language Haiku.* Winchester, Va.: Red Moon Press, 2001, 9.

11. Jerry Kilbride, in Jim Kacian and the Red Moon editorial staff, editors. *Tug of the Current: The Red Moon Anthology of English-Language Haiku.* Winchester, Va.: Red Moon Press, 2005, 42.

our bodies as we grow older. We simply cannot escape the body and changes associated with aging or sickness.

autumn wind
I compare my hair
with Rapunzel's[12]

her only nipple
begins to harden
a new year[13]

Birthdays, of course, can be a bittersweet reminder:

another birthday
I push the candles in
deeper[14]

These same issues are present in our relationships with lovers and friends, parents and children. A common lament among parents is that their children grow up too quickly; before one knows it, the children have become adults. Friendships, too, are subject to disruption.

12. Fay Aoyagi, in *Mariposa* 13 (autumn–winter 2005).
13. Vincent Tripi, in Jim Kacian and the Red Moon editorial staff, editors. *Edge of Light: The Red Moon Anthology of English-Language Haiku*. Winchester, Va.: Red Moon Press, 2004. 87.
14. Penny Harter, in Kacian et al. *Edge of Light*, 40.

in my wallet
my daughter still
thirteen[15]

California friends—
here today
gone today.[16]

Warhol understood that the prospect of death underlies the passing—the endless passing—of moments. Death, the "ancient enemy," is the one inevitability we all must face.[17] This prospect can make us feel, as paul m. notes, that we live on borrowed time.

summer's end—
riding a borrowed bicycle
past the graveyard[18]

In contrast to the feeling of "borrowedness" of life, death seems final and permanent. Even if we believe in an afterlife or reincarnation, we understand that we are leaving this life and this world as we have experienced it and know it.

15. John Kinory, in Jim Kacian and the Red Moon editorial staff, editors. *Inside the Mirror: The 2005 Red Moon Anthology of English-Language Haiku.* Winchester, Va.: Red Moon Press, 2006, 39.
16. Alexis Rotella, in Ross. *How to Haiku*, 42.
17. Koch, *Stargazer*, 134.
18. paul m. [Paul Miller]. *Finding the Way: Haiku and Field Notes.* Foster City, Calif.: Press Here, 2002.

a gust of wind
the gravestone's shadow
doesn't move[19]

fallen headstone
the letters
fill with rain[20]

Like Warhol, haiku writers engage with questions surrounding mortality and the impermanence of life. Koch notes, "Immediacy, especially in the great traditions of the Romantic movement, is always on the edge of death somewhere because we're always losing the moment. It's always vanishing."

gone from the woods
the bird I knew
by song alone[21]

19. Ibid.
20. w.f. owen, in Kacian et al. *Inside the Mirror*, 56.
21. Paul O. Williams. *The Nick of Time: Essays on Haiku Aesthetics*. Edited and introduced by Lee Gurga and Michael Dylan Welch. Foster City, Calif.: Press Here, 2001, 76.

"Glossy Black Painting":
Notes on Modern Art and Haiku

During the years 1951-1953, Robert Rauschenberg created a breakthrough series of work known as the "Black Paintings." One of these, *Untitled* (*Glossy Black Painting*), reminds the viewer that modern art and haiku share important elements, and even a common approach.

The painting consists of numerous 2 to 4-inch torn and/or crinkled newspaper clippings sprinkled across a roughly 4.5 by 6-foot canvas. The entire work—canvas and newspaper fragments—is coated with glossy black paint. The composition contains no obvious imagery: no scenery, no characters, and no objects (besides the unreadable newspaper fragments). It is simply a spacious surface textured with newspaper and painted black.

The painting's lack of obvious imagery, its monochrome nature, and its lack of a title mean that the viewer is not explicitly provided a meaning. If the observer wants a meaning, he or she must actively participate in constructing that meaning, either drawing upon their own experiences or learning about the motives of the artist. In this way, *Glossy Black Painting* is similar to many haiku.

Also like many haiku, which depict everyday experiences, *Glossy Black Painting* features an everyday material (newspaper) and eschews "showy" or "artsy" components.

These similarities are not a coincidence. Rauschenberg was influenced by the composer John Cage, who was interested in Zen Buddhism.[1] Rauschenberg incorporated into his work some of Cage's Buddhist-influenced ideas, including the assimilation of external factors (i.e. allowing the observer to participate).[2]

Rauschenberg hoped that the "Black Paintings" (along with related work) would break down traditional conceptions of art and challenge viewers to see in new ways. The values he turned to were already present in haiku. For haiku writers, *Glossy Black Painting* underscores the relevance of haiku and reminds us that the form still has a critical, eye-opening mission.

---

1. Mattison, Robert S. *Robert Rauschenberg: Breaking Boundaries*. New Haven and London: Yale University Press, 2003: 52.

2. Tischler, Barbara L. "John Cage." *The Reader's Companion to American History*. Eric Foner and John A. Garraty (editors). Boston: Houghton Mifflin Company, 1991. Web edition: http://college.hmco.com/history/readerscomp/rcah/html/rc_013600_cagejohn.htm.

"The Inspiration of a Moment": Calder's Mobiles and Haiku

The similarities between haiku and modern art have long been recognized.[1] One intriguing case is that of Alexander Calder and his famous mobiles. At first glance, Calder's mobiles seem a world apart from haiku. Upon closer inspection, however, it becomes apparent that they share important qualities.

Calder's mobiles are among the most recognized icons of twentieth-century modern art. They have been influential not only in the arts but in other fields such as interior design and toy making. Ranging in scope from small table pieces to outdoor monuments, Calder's mobiles are kinetic sculptures that are designed to be affected by the elements—to be stirred and moved by the wind, ground vibrations, and even temperature changes.

Commonalities with haiku start with the sheer brevity of Calder's approach. In haiku, of course, brevity takes the form of the small number of words used in the poem. Similarly, in Calder's work, a key element of concision is the small number of

1. The connection has been noted in various places. For an example, see "From Bashō to Barthes," by Lee Gurga, appearing in *Hermitage: A Haiku Journal*, Volume 1, Numbers 1-2 (Summer-Winter 2004): 65-77. Also, see my article "'Glossy Black Painting': Notes on Modern Art and Haiku," which appeared in *Mariposa* 13 (Autumn-Winter 2005).

constituents that make up the sculpture. There are many pieces that exemplify this principle; a notable example is his largest mobile, "La Spirale." Housed on the grounds of the UNESCO building in Paris, "La Spirale" is thirty feet high. It is constructed of painted steel, and is composed of a stable base that supports six wind-driven, cantilevered mobile triangular plates.[2] The plates spin and spiral in the wind. Despite its monumental stature, the entire piece is composed of just a handful of objects—the six plates and their supporting parts.

The small number of constituents compels the viewer to hone in on what Calder believes to be important—in this case, how spirals work. By being judicious with the number of building blocks, Calder is able to distill the essence of a thing—not only concrete objects like plants and animals but also abstract processes like spirals.[3]

The brevity of Calder's approach is also manifested through the simplicity of the shapes that he used to build mobiles. He often used basic shapes like circles and triangles (which offer the benefit of fluid movement through space), and typically resorted to using just a few colors—chiefly

2. Howard Greenfeld. *The Essential Alexander Calder*. New York: The Wonderland Press, 2003: 92-93.
3. For examples of animals and plants, see "Hen," "Elephant Head," "Yellow Whale," and "Sword Plant." Each of these is viewable at The Calder Foundation website at http://www.calder.org/ (as of July 2, 2006).

red, yellow and blue.[4] Like haiku, Calder eschewed overly complex building blocks. Calder also kept his construction techniques relatively simple: he typically used a few tools that he could carry easily when traveling.[5]

Besides brevity, Calder's work with mobiles also shares with haiku a foundation in nature. This may not be noticeable at first glance since Calder's works are so obviously built of manufactured materials like aluminum and steel. Nature is a key element in Calder's mobiles. Animals are subjects of many pieces — so much so that together they are categorized as "animobiles."[6] The insect world, plants and natural processes are common subjects as well, with pieces inspired by leaves, spiders and even snow flurries.

Even more fundamentally, Calder's mobiles are intended to interact with, and be affected by, the natural world. Jean-Paul Sartre, who coined the term "mobiles," explains: "What they may do at a given moment will be determined by the time of day, the sun, the temperature or the wind. The object is thus always half way between the servility of a statue and the independence of natural events; each of its evolutions is the inspiration of a

4. Jean Lipman. *Calder's Universe*. New York: The Whitney Museum of American Art, 1976: 264.
5. Ibid, 265.
6. Ibid, 262.

moment."[7] Like haiku, Calder's mobiles respond to the environment—and also change from moment to moment. As Sartre notes, "Valéry said of the sea that it is a perpetual recommencement. A 'mobile' is in this way like the sea, and is equally enchanting: forever re-beginning, forever new."[8]

Finally, like much modern art generally, Calder's mobiles demand that the viewer participate in interpreting—constructing—the meaning of the artwork. A typical example would be "Polygones Noirs."[9] This piece is in the classic look of Calder's hanging mobiles, resembling a toy mobile used for infants. It hangs by a wire from the ceiling and is composed of several polygonal shapes that move and spin. What does "Polygones Noirs" mean? Does it mean anything? In order to arrive at an answer, the viewer must either contribute to that meaning or learn more about the context of the work and its creator.

One difference between Calder's philosophy and the haiku way is that Calder's approach to nature is more intellectual and theoretical—that is, more removed—than haiku. Describing his

7. Jean-Paul Sartre, "The Mobiles of Calder." Preface to an exhibition in Paris, 1946. Essay appears on The Calder Foundation website at http://www.calder.org/ (as of July 2, 2006).
8. Ibid.
9. Jean Lipman. *Calder's Universe.* New York: The Whitney Museum of American Art, 1976: 296-7. I also discussed this point in the aforementioned essay in *Mariposa* 13. See footnote 1.

approach, Calder noted, "The basis of everything for me is the universe."[10] Explaining the origin of this, he related, "The first inspiration I ever had was the cosmos, the planetary system. My mother used to say to me, 'But you don't know anything about the stars.' I'd say, 'No, I don't, but you can have an idea what they're like without knowing all about them and shaking hands with them.'"[11] This approach is fundamentally different than the direct, experiential approach of haiku.

Like other modern artists, important parts of Calder's oeuvre share a similar approach with haiku. In Calder's case, commonalities include brevity and simplicity; inspiration from nature; and an interactive relationship between the artwork and the viewer. These similarities afford haiku writers and readers a doorway into Calder's art and the study of it—or, simply the enjoyment of it.

10. Howard Greenfeld. *The Essential Alexander Calder*. New York: The Wonderland Press, 2003: 19.
11. Jean Lipman. *Calder's Universe*. New York: The Whitney Museum of American Art, 1976: 17.

SIMPLE INGREDIENTS:
NEW YORKER COVER ART AND HAIKU

Few magazines possess cover art as iconic as that of the *New Yorker*. Since the 1920s, *New Yorker* covers have amused, enlightened and, occasionally, offended readers. The famous 1976 "View from Manhattan" cover, for example, satirized the view that some New Yorkers held of "flyover" states.[1] More recently, the "Politics of Fear" cover—which depicted Barack and Michelle Obama in traditional Islamic and "Black Power" garb, respectively—generated a firestorm of controversy during the 2008 presidential election.[2]

Beyond the blockbusters, however, *New Yorker* cover art often focuses on more quotidian matter. While naturally ranging in style and intent, much of the cover art focuses on everyday life—and approaches this matter in ways surprisingly similar to haiku.

The vignettes portrayed on the magazine's covers are often rooted in, and attuned to, the seasons. In a March issue, for example, the cover depicts a woman sitting in an armchair by the window, contentedly reading a newspaper.[3] A

---

1. Saul Steinberg, in *The New Yorker*, March 29, 1976.
2. Barry Blitt, in *The New Yorker*, July 21, 2008.
3. James Stevenson, in *The New Yorker*, March 15, 1976.

flowerpot on the window sill has sprouted a flower that has spread fantastically over the entire room. The plant embodies the vibrancy and playfulness associated with spring.

> lilacs in bloom
> a swallowtail crosses
> the double-yellow line[4]

An April cover, entitled "Lost and Found,"[5] has as its subject a quintessential spring topic, baseball. As Allan Burns notes, a new baseball season is as "sure a sign of spring as the return of avian migrants and the budding of leaves."[6] The *New Yorker* cover shows the outstretched arm of a baseball player (an outfielder), his glove closing around a baseball. Only the player's arm is visible: While the player has caught the ball, he has run into the outfield wall and his body is shrouded in the thick ivy that carpets the wall. The player's go-for-broke attitude matches the enthusiasm of fans delighted that the baseball season has arrived and also reflects the enthusiasm that the first warm weather triggers.

---

4. Jack Barry, *Swamp Candles* (Down-to-Earth Books, 2006).
5. Mark Ulriksen, in *The New Yorker*, April 7, 2008.
6. Allan Burns, "Play Ball": Montage #5, The Haiku Foundation website, http://thehaikufoundation.org/montage/montage_2009_04_05.pdf.

spring breeze
this grassy field makes me
want to play catch[7]

The two spring vignettes work in much the same way as haiku. Each focuses on a single moment, and each employs a seasonal motif to articulate the feeling. In fact, the motifs (a flower, baseball) perform the same function as kigo: "pictorial kigo" or "visual kigo" we might term them. They are a marker to the viewer about the time of year and the events and activities—and sentiments—associated with it.

At the other end of the year, the cover for a December issue depicts a man carrying a large Christmas tree through the revolving door of his apartment building. The tree is almost too large to fit through the door, and the man is anxiously squeezing it through.[8] Of course, New Yorkers, many of whom live in tight quarters, want to celebrate the holiday as everyone does. The artist reminds us that even in big cities, seasonal milestones and rhythms remain important.

7. Masaoka Shiki, in *Baseball Haiku: American and Japanese Haiku and Senryu on Baseball*, ed. Cor van den Heuvel and Nanae Tamura (New York: W. W. Norton & Company, 2007), 143.
8. Charles Saxon, in *The New Yorker*, December 20, 1976.

winter commute
my hand finds a warm spot
on the handrail[9]

Each of these covers also employs the use of suggestion—another hallmark of haiku. Unlike more descriptive art, these compositions suggest or imply meanings, rather than directly and explicitly doing so. The artists offer a compelling image and a dash of innuendo. It's up to the viewer to finish the thought.

Of course, the "wordlessness" of the format logically compels the practice of suggestion. Unlike, say, the cartoons in the magazine (which normally include captions), the covers are more evocative and less explicit.

An important benefit to hewing close to the seasons and to quotidian (in contrast to topical) matter is longevity. The first spring cover described above—that of the flower pot—was published in 1976. Its simplicity is as effective today as it was over thirty years ago.

The constituents of the covers—roots in seasonality, a focus on the moment, the practice of suggestion—are present throughout the history of the magazine. The success of *New Yorker* cover art represents the success of its ingredients—the same ingredients that form the basis of haiku.

---

9. Dee Evetts, *endgrain* (Winchester, VA: Red Moon Press, 1997).

HAIKU AND SENRYU

Halloween party—
after a few drinks
the masks come off

afternoon sun
moves across the board—
bishop to d8

working late
corrido norteño
from the elevator

layoffs—
the indents from the chair
still in the carpet

balancing the checkbook
again
cold coffee

buying another
lotto ticket—
moonless night

the coldness
of my pocket change—
cardboard shelter

packing—
the weight
of empty boxes

hospital waiting room
the steadiness
of the air conditioner

you leave—
the deeper blue
of dusk

RELIGIOUS TRADITION AND HAIKU: NOTES ON TAOISM AND HAIKU

There's been a lot of discussion in recent years about the relationship between Zen and haiku. I've found less focus on one of Zen's forebears, Taoism. I think that the topic of Taoism and haiku deserves some attention; as Robert Spiess noted, "One of the historical aspects of haiku is that of Taoism . . ."[1]

The *Tao Te Ching* opens with the declaration:

> "The tao that can be told
> is not the eternal Tao.
> The name that can be named
> is not the eternal Name."[2]

Spiess writes that "entities in haiku are presented in their unadorned naturalness."[3] The *shasei* (objective/realist) approach has been predominant in classic haiku and much contemporary American haiku. Through a focus on the everyday world, haiku poets hope to peek into the ultimate reality. As William Carlos Williams famously wrote, "No

---

1. Robert Spiess, *A Year's Speculations on Haiku* (Madison, WI: Modern Haiku, 1995), January twenty-ninth.
2. *Tao Te Ching*, tr. Stephen Mitchell (New York: HarperPerennial, 2006), Ch. 1.
3. Spiess, *Speculations*, January twenty-ninth.

ideas but in things." Fidelity to things, as they are, is a door through which the conscientious can possibly glimpse the unnameable Name.

> They end their flight
> one by one—
> crows at dusk.
> —Buson[4]

Paul Williams observed that strong haiku are often born from our daily lives: "such perceptions as do transform themselves into haiku tend to emerge from the familiar rather than the new."[5] This is in line with the *Tao Te Ching*: "Thus the Master travels all day / without leaving home."[6] Of course, this is not meant to be a literal injunction against travel or new experiences. Rather, it is a recognition that effective insights often grow out of seeing the same things in a new light.

4. *The Essential Haiku: Versions of Bashō, Buson, & Issa*, tr. Robert Hass (New Jersey: The Ecco Press, 1994), 89.
5. Paul O. Williams, "Loafing Alertly: Observation and Haiku," in *The Nick of Time: Essays on Haiku Aesthetics*, eds. Lee Gurga and Michael Dylan Welch (Foster City, CA: Press Here, 2001), 21.
6. *Tao*, Ch. 26.

the golden sunset
i lay waiting on my board
for the perfect wave
                —Bruce Feingold[7]

Lao-tzu said: "We shape clay into a pot, / but it is the emptiness inside / that holds whatever we want."[8] Haiku's brevity and the practice of suggestion—the spaces before, between, and after the words—are ways into Lao-tzu's emptiness.

listening to
the ocean's history—
spring sunset
                —Fay Aoyagi[9]

One of the objectives of Taoism is to teach people how to conduct their lives and live in harmony with the Tao. Practices like Tai Chi and mediation are designed to help. For haiku poets, the notion of "creative quietude," as Huston Smith terms it, is relevant. Smith describes how "genuine creation, as every artist knows, comes when the more abundant resources of the subliminal self are somehow

7. Bruce Feingold, *A New Moon* (Winchester, VA: Red Moon Press, 2004), 58.
8. *Tao*, Ch. 11.
9. Fay Aoygai, *In Borrowed Shoes* (San Francisco: Blue Willow Press), 4.

tapped."[10] This, of course, is challenging but satisfying to achieve.

> wind-shaped trees
> a young hawk
> measures the sky
> —paul m.[11]

10. Huston Smith, *The World's Religions: Our Great Wisdom Traditions* (New York: HarperSanFrancisco, 1991), 208.
11. paul m., *finding the way: haiku and field notes* (Foster City, CA: Press Here, 2002).

Religious Tradition and Haiku: Unity

The creation story in the Hebrew Bible is well known: God created the heaven and the earth in six days. Curiously, there is a second creation story in Judaism, this one from the Kabbalistic tradition. When God created the world, He needed to make space to do so; after all, God was everything. In order to make the world, God withdrew "in all directions away from one point at the center of its infinity, as it were, thereby creating a vacuum. This vacuum served as the site of creation."[1]

Of course, God did not withdraw completely. The divine presence remained ubiquitous, tying everything together. Underneath the surface distinctness of things, an essential unity is the immutable reality. The *Koran* says, "Wheresoever you turn, there is the face of Allah."[2] Buddhists bring their palms together to represent overcoming surface duality.[3]

---

1. Daniel Matt, *The Essential Kabbalah: The Heart of Jewish Mysticism* (New York: HarperSanFrancisco, 1995), 15.
2. James Fadiman and Robert Frager, eds., *Essential Sufism* (New York: HarperSanFrancisco, 1999), 228.
3. Huston Smith, *The World's Religions: Our Great Wisdom Traditions* (New York: HarperSanFrancisco, 1991), 388.

downpour:
my "I-Thou"
T-shirt
　　　—Raymond Roseliep[4]

Grounded in the natural world, the interdependence of all things—living and non-living—is a theme of many contemporary haiku.

out of the hermit thrush
out of the valley
one song
　　　—Laurie Stoelting[5]

As K. Ramesh notes, we sometimes become aware of this reality in the most unlikely of places.

dusk—
a chatter of frogs outside
the teacher's house[6]

R. H. Blyth wrote that haiku is imbued with "that state of mind in which we are not separated from other things, are indeed identical with them, and

4. Cor van den Heuvel, ed., *The Haiku Anthology* (New York: W. W. Norton & Company, 1999), 163.
5. Laurie Stoelting, *Light on the Mountain: Selections*, ed. Vincent Tripi (Greenfield, MA: Tribe Press, 2008).
6. K. Ramesh, *Soap Bubbles: Haiku* (Winchester, VA: Red Moon Press, 2007).

yet retain our own individuality and personal peculiarities."[7] Haiku offers us—as readers and poets—the joy of experiencing this reality. We appreciate and delight in the unique ways that other poets experience this—and reflect on the ways that we ourselves do.

---

7. R. H. Blyth, *Haiku: Eastern Culture* (Hokuseido, 1960), iii.

RELIGIOUS TRADITION AND HAIKU: MYSTERY

Religion tells us that the world is grounded in mystery—and cannot be wholly understood rationally or empirically. The Muslim scholar Muhammad Asad wrote, "Man is unable to explain to himself the mystery of life, the mystery of birth and death, the mystery of infinity and eternity."[1]

> pulling light
> from the other world . . .
> the Milky Way
> —Yatsuka Ishihara[2]

Flannery O'Connor wrote that the aim of writing is to embody this mystery.[3] We need not venture far to be touched by the experience; small daily events can open the door to us.

---

1. Muhammad Asad, *Islam at the Crossroads* (Gibraltar: Dar al-Andalus Ltd, 1982), 3.
2. Yatsuka Ishihara, *Red Fuji: Selected Haiku of Yatsuka Ishihara*, trans. and ed. Tadashi Kondo and William Higginson (Santa Fe: From Here Press, 1997), 73.
3. Flannery O'Connor, *Mystery and Manners: Occasional Prose*, ed. Sally Fitzgerald and Robert Fitzgerald (New York: Farrar, Straus & Giroux, 2001), 124.

how deer
materialize
twilight
—Scott Mason[4]

Mason appreciates how the deer seems to materialize from nowhere—as if by magic. He appreciates the unique, inbred skill of the animal. One can imagine the questions that follow such an encounter: How was this marvelous animal created? What about the countless other creatures in this world? For that matter, how was the world created?

Of course, the twentieth and twenty-first centuries have seen immense advances in science. Some have observed that modernity and science have predisposed us against mystery. But science, while shedding light on many unknowns, at the same time offers new avenues of wonder about the nature of life and the universe.

Venus and
the praying mantis
born from the foam
—Takenami Akira[5]

4. *A New Resonance 6: Emerging Voices in English-Language Haiku,* ed. Jim Kacian and Dee Evetts (Winchester, VA: Red Moon Press, 2009), 109.
5. Takenami Akira. World Haiku Association website. http://www.worldhaiku.net/poetry/jp/a.takenami/a.takenami.htm. Accessed September 9, 2010.

Religious Tradition and Haiku: Grace

The dictionary defines "grace" as "the freely given, unmerited favor and love of god."[1] The *Koran* says: "Let the People of the Book recognize that they have no control over the grace of God; that grace is in His hands alone, and that He vouchsafes it to whom He will."[2]

One form of grace originates in nature. This is not surprising as the natural world is the creation or manifestation of divinity.

> In these latter-day,
> Degenerate times,
> Cherry-blossoms everywhere!
> — Issa[3]

Issa recognizes that whatever people may do, the natural world offers solace, or a reprieve. It's important to note that Issa explicitly acknowledges that the gifts of nature are offered to all people, irrespective of their character—and whether their actions be virtuous or "degenerate."

Grace can also be transmitted from fellow human beings—family and friends, acquaintances and strangers.

---

1. http://dictionary.reference.com/browse/grace. Accessed August 7, 2010.
2. *The Koran: With Parallel Arabic Text* (London: Penguin Books, 2000), 540.
3. R. H. Blyth, *Haiku: Spring (Volume II)* (Hokuseido, 1960), 346.

Christmas Eve—
under the car's hood
a stranger
　　　—Glenn Coats[4]

Grace is an immensely popular concept—and no wonder. Because, from our perspective, there is no discernible logic to it, the idea encourages us to approach the world in an open, receptive way. We cannot know when we will be visited by grace. We await those moments when we—irrespective of everything—experience the gift.

---

4. *A New Resonance 6: Emerging Voices in English-Language Haiku*, ed. Jim Kacian and Dee Evetts (Winchester, VA: Red Moon Press, 2009), 24.

RELIGIOUS TRADITION AND HAIKU: RITUAL

Ritual is ubiquitous in religion. Mention any religion, and a ritual is usually the first image that comes to mind. Rituals are closely tied to family and community; they also mark the seasons and the passing of time. For these reasons, they continue to be important not just to the segment of practicing believers but also the broader public.

> Ash Wednesday foreheads
> here and there
> in the financial district
> —Tom Tico[1]

> Christmas Eve
> the last wisp of smoke
> from the blown-out candle
> —Michael Ketchek[2]

When we miss these observances, we feel the loss.

> Tanabata festival
> weaving at home
> alone
> —Tatsuki Matsutani[3]

1. Tom Tico, *Modern Haiku* 41:2, 14.
2. Michael Ketchek, *Modern Haiku* 40:3, 58.
3. Tatsuki Matsutani, *Modern Haiku* 41:1, 56.

Festival of Souls
probably no water for them
in the cemetery this year
　　—Yotenchi Agari[4]

From a practical point of view, rituals can seem arbitrary and extraneous: window dressing when compared to the substance of religious ideas. However, ritual performs a key function, helping us manage life transitions. Huston Smith writes: "Death is the glaring example. Stunned by tragic bereavement, we would founder completely if we were thrown on our own and had to think our way through the ordeal. This is why death, with its funerals and memorial services, its wakes and sitting shiva, is the most ritualized rite of passage."[5]

bouquet of daisies
　　a bee comes to visit
　　my mother's grave
　　　—Christoper Herold[6]

Of course, rituals are rooted in the past. But rituals are also dynamic, changing over time and

4. Yotenchi Agari, *Modern Haiku* 40:2, 59. Quoted from Margaret Chula's essay, "Behind Barbed Wire: Haiku from the Internment Camps."
5. Huston Smith, *The World's Religions: Our Great Wisdom Traditions* (New York: HarperSanFrancisco, 1991), 300-301.
6. Christopher Herold, *Mariposa* 12.

adapting to new realities: everything from new technology to more diverse audiences.

> Chicago's grotto of Lourdes—
> an electric switch
> lights a candle for my father
> —Mary L. Kwas[7]

> late mourners
> the rabbi switches
> from Hebrew to English
> —Michael Dylan Welch[8]

In large and small ways, each of us can turn to our tradition, and be enveloped in its warm embrace.

> Chinese New Year
> recent immigrants
> carrying the dragon
> —Patrick Gallagher[9]

---

7. Mary L. Kwas, *Modern Haiku* 40:2, 64.
8. Michael Dylan Welch, *Modern Haiku* 39:1, 88.
9. Patrick Gallagher, *Mariposa* 16.

RELIGIOUS TRADITION AND HAIKU:
HAIKU AS PRAYER

The early Sufi master, Ansari of Herat, tells a story about Ali, the son-in-law of the Prophet. During a battle, Ali was shot in the leg by an arrow. To remove it, it was necessary to make a painful incision. Ali's family asked that the operation wait until Ali started praying because then he would be totally unconscious of the world around him. Indeed, when finished with his prayers, Ali wondered why the pain in his leg had diminished.[1]

Mary Karr has described poetry as "sacred speech."[2] Indeed, poetry has often been compared to prayer. Both poetry and prayer can remove us from our focus on daily routine, and usher in a different state of mind. Jane Hirshfield writes, "Poetry's work is the clarification and magnification of being. Each time we enter its word-woven and musical invocation, we give ourselves over to a different mode of knowing . . ."[3]

---

1. James Fadiman and Robert Frager, eds., *Essential Sufism* (New York: HarperSanFrancisco, 1997), 207.
2. Mary Karr, "Facing Altars: Poetry and Prayer" (*Poetry*, November 2005). http://www.poetryfoundation.org/poetrymagazine/article/175809 (Accessed April 14, 2011).
3. Jane Hirshfield, *Nine Gates: Entering the Mind of Poetry* (New York: HarperPerennial, 1997), vii.

morning prayers—
the blind nun
closes her eyes
　　　—George Dorsty[4]

missed my mind
by this much—
Zen archery
　　　—Stanford Forrester[5]

Of course, there are many ways to engage in prayer: song, dance, silence . . .

silent Friends meeting . . .
the sound of chairs being moved
to enlarge the circle
　　　—Robert Major[6]

People resort to prayer for a variety of reasons: petition, confession, contemplation, thanksgiving, and more. Even for the devoted, sometimes doubt creeps in:

---

4. George Dorsty, *inside the mirror: The Red Moon Anthology*, ed. Jim Kacian (Winchester, VA: Red Moon Press, 2006), 22.
5. Stanford Forrester, *Mariposa* 18 (Spring/Summer 2008).
6. Robert Major, *refuge* (Winchester, VA: Red Moon Press, 2008). Originally published in *The Heron's Nest* (IV:8).

River Baptism
for those of us not sure
the rain starts
    —Garry Gay[7]

In all cases, prayer and haiku require receptiveness and openness—even, for example, to a disruption during a somber event:

at the open grave
mingling with the priest's prayer:
honking of wild geese
    —Nick Virgilio[8]

7. Garry Gay, *Mariposa* 12 (Spring/Summer 2005).
8. Nick Virgilio, *The Haiku Anthology*, ed. Cor van den Heuvel (New York: W. W. Norton & Company, 1999), 264.

HAIKU AND SENRYU

the hawk also waiting
for shadows—
Groundhog Day

the darkness meows
for food
winter night

street corner memorial—
my four-year-old
asks for the balloon

the morning's first raindrops
plop into the dust—
news from Karbala

memorial candle
the smoke
turning into air

roadside cross
a blur—
winter evening

flat tire at the summit—
my son's first glimpse
of the Milky Way

Sistine Chapel
a young boy
plays with his shoelaces

two cigarettes
left on the windowsill—
winter stars

choosing a Christmas tree—
the kids think
every one is perfect

The Eye of the Storm: Micropoems

"I have made this [letter] longer than usual, only because I have not had the time to make it shorter."
—Blaise Pascal[1]

During the nineteen-eighties and nineties, the San Francisco transit system featured poetry and literary broadsides on its buses and streetcars. One day, while engrossed in *Moby Dick*, I glanced overhead and noticed a broadside of the poem "El Hombre" by William Carlos Williams:[2]

It's a strange courage
you give me ancient star:

Shine alone in the sunrise
toward which you lend no part!

Though I had been reading and studying Moby Dick for several weeks, Williams' one-sentence poem intrigued me. And ultimately, it has left a more lasting impression than Melville's voluminous book. Like an old folk proverb, the poem has dispensed a wisdom far out of proportion to its length.

1. Blaise Pascal, "Lettres Provinciales," no. 16, 1657. *The Oxford Dictionary of Quotations*, ed. Elizabeth Knowles (Oxford: Oxford University Press, 1999): 568.
2. William Carlos Williams, "El Hombre." *William Carlos Williams: Selected Poems*, ed. Charles Tomlinson (New York: New Directions Books, 1985): 20.

"El Hombre" has not been the exception. Many short poems—with their characteristic "knockout" epiphanies—have left strong imprints on my consciousness and memory.

> I go
> you stay;
>   two autumns.
> —Shiki[3]

The adjectives "short" and "brief" don't seem to do justice to the condensed clarity of many short poems. They seem to be almost "micro" poems.

These "micropoems" come from many traditions and appear in many forms. There are the verses of the ancient Chinese poets Tu Fu and Li Po. The haiku of Bashō, Buson, Issa, and Shiki come out of a unique intellectual tradition. Modern Western poets—Wallace Stevens, Antonio Machado, and Thomas McGrath, for instance—write short poems as different as apples and oranges. Despite this diversity, however, there is nevertheless a distinct set of qualities found in micropoems.

---

3. Shiki, "I go." Tr. Robert Hass. *The Essential Haiku: Versions of Bashō, Buson, and Issa,* ed. Robert Hass (Hopewell, New Jersey: Ecco Press, 1994): 81. Note: Robert Hass attributes this haiku to Buson, but Shiki was the author. See: Burton Watson, *Masaoka Shiki: Selected Poems* (New York: Columbia University Press, 1998).

It's reasonable to expect that the tight format—the narrow "wiggle room"—of micropoems would reify into a straitjacket, but there are in fact a wonderful variety of short poems. Of course, the most popular type is the haiku:

> Above the boat,
> bellies
> of wild geese.

The goal of haiku, including this classic by Kikaku,[4] is to simply capture a moment in nature and to imply its significance for the reader. Along with its "twin" genre senryu—which is identical to haiku except that it deals wholly with the human sphere, not nature—haiku compels us to notice the everyday world.

In this sense, the task of a haiku poet is like that of a photographer. A photographer captures a moment on film in such a way that the viewer is compelled to react in the same way the photographer was stimulated to. For example, Dorothea Lange's famous photo of a mother and son, Oakie migrant farmworkers, captures a moment and stimulates the viewer to see the significance Lange observed.

---

4. Kikaku, "Above the boat ..." Tr. Lucien Stryk and Takashi Ikemoto. *A Book of Luminous Things: An International Anthology of Poetry*, ed. Czeslaw Milosz (New York: Harcourt Brace & Company, 1996): 6.

In its purest form, haiku avoids "handing" the meaning to the reader; rather, the haiku poet seeks to recreate the circumstances so the reader experiences a similar response.

> I look into a dragonfly's eye
> and see
> the mountains over my shoulder.[5]

The Japanese poet Issa notices that he can see the mountains in an insect's eye; he leaves it to the reader to react to this. Of course, the moments that the poet selects to record are chosen for a reason; the very choice of a moment suggests an interpretation. But the haiku, more than any other genre, leaves that interpretation to the reader. Cor van den Heuvel, editor of *The Haiku Anthology*, writes, "the reader must share in the creative process, being willing to associate and pick up on the echoes implicit in the words. A wrong focus, or lack of awareness, and he will see only a closed door."[6] Roland Barthes observes: "neither describing, nor defining, the haiku diminishes to the point of pure and sole designation."[7] Haiku is successful when it

5. Issa, "I look into a dragonfly's eye ..." tr. Robert Bly. *The Sea and the Honeycomb: A Book of Tiny Poems*, ed. Robert Bly (Boston: Beacon Press, 1971): 47.
6. Cor van den Heuvel, ed. *The Haiku Anthology: Haiku and Senryu in English* (3rd ed.) (New York: W. W. Norton, 1999): xv–xvi.
7. Roland Barthes, *Empire of Signs*, tr. Richard Howard (New York: Hill and Wang, 1982), 83.

"designates" a moment—isolates it so the reader notices and responds.

Many poets have moved a step beyond the "moment-capture" of haiku to a more explicit declaration of meaning. Octavio Paz's "Boy and Top" explicitly declares a meaning, and therefore is only masquerading as a haiku:

> Each time he flings it
> it falls, just,
> in the center of the world.[8]

A haiku poet might say that the top falls in the middle of the floor, or on the table, or wherever it happens to fall. Paz, however, declares that it falls in "the center of the world," thereby making a statement about humanity's place in the cosmos.

Adam Zagajewski's "Auto Mirror" also defines the response for the reader:

> In the rear-view mirror suddenly
> I saw the bulk of the Beauvais Cathedral;
> great things dwell in small ones
> for a moment.[9]

8. Octavio Paz, "Boy and Top." *The Haiku Handbook: How to Write, Share, and Teach Haiku*, William J. Higginson and Penny Harter (Tokyo: Kodansha International, 1989): 60.

9. Adam Zagajewski, "Auto Mirror." Tr. Czeslaw Milosz and Robert Hass. *A Book of Luminous Things: An International Anthology of Poetry*, ed. Czeslaw Milosz (New York: Harcourt Brace & Company, 1996): 128.

Though "Auto Mirror" shares a few characteristics with haiku—for example, it presents an unexpected moment—it in fact diverges from the haiku aesthetic. In haiku, the last two lines would be considered redundant: they repeat literally what the first two lines show figuratively. Unlike haiku, it could be argued that Zagajewski's poem doesn't trust the reader to respond on his or her own.

Moving away from haiku, Bertolt Brecht's "Changing the Wheel" also explicitly declares a meaning:

> I sit by the roadside
> The driver changes the wheel.
> I do not like the place I have come from.
> I do not like the place I am going to.
> Why with impatience do I
> Watch him changing the wheel?[10]

Brecht's rhetorical question, of course, gives an answer of sorts. The next logical step in the chain is to discard the "moment" altogether, and issue a statement of truth.

> It is good knowing that glasses
> are to drink from;

10. Bertolt Brecht, "Changing the Wheel." Tr. Michael Hamburger. *The Poetry of Survival: Post-War Poets of Central and Eastern Europe*, ed. Daniel Weissbort (London: Penguin Books, 1993): 33.

the bad thing is not to know
what thirst is for.[11]

Antonio Machado's poem sounds like a proverb. In fact, Machado entitled the set to which this quatrain belonged "Proverbs and Songs." Francisco Alarcón accomplishes the same goal as Machado—declaring a truth—but does so without sounding like a proverb in his poem "We're One":

sea
dust
tear
pollen[12]

There are several forms that are related to the "proverb-poem" genre. Epigrams have existed at least since *The Greek Anthology* (ca. 700 BC–1000 AD) and enjoyed a renaissance during the neo-classical period in England, popularized by John Donne, Ben Jonson, and Alexander Pope. Compact and clever, epigrams often seek to make a point through playful wit, as does this classic from Pope's "An Essay on Criticism":[13]

11. Antonio Machado, "It is good knowing that glasses." Tr. Robert Bly. *Times Alone: Selected Poems of Antonio Machado*, ed. Robert Bly (Hanover, New Hampshire: Wesleyan University Press, 1983): 111.
12. Francisco X. Alarcón, "We're One." *Snake Poems: An Aztec Invocation* (San Francisco: Chronicle Books, 1992): 114.
13. Alexander Pope, from "An Essay on Criticism." *Alexander Pope: Selected*

Authors are partial to their wit, 'tis true,
But are not Critics to their judgment too?

Another genre related to both the proverb-poem and the epigram is the riddle, exemplified in this two-line poem by Joseph Brodsky:[14]

Sir, you are tough, and I am tough.
But who will write whose epitaph?

A cousin of the riddle is the "joke" poem. The best jokes, in poetry and in their own right, have always exposed truths about human nature and society. Senryu is renowned for its humor. Limericks are a popularized form of humorous poetry. Thomas McGrath's "For the Critic Who Tries to Write Poems" is funny and reveals something about the creative process:[15]

Well, well little poet
still trying to find a dew drop
in the middle of a thunderstorm!

Poetry, ed. Douglas Grant (London: Penguin Books, 1985): 14.

14. Joseph Brodsky, "Sir, You are Tough." *Poetry in Motion: 100 Poems from the Subways and Buses*, eds. Molly Peacock, Elise Paschen, and Neil Neches (New York & London: W. W. Norton, 1996): 29.

15. Thomas McGrath, "For a Critic Who Tries to Write Poems." *Passages Toward the Dark* (Port Townsend, Washington: Copper Canyon Press, 1982): 71.

Thom Gunn's two-line observation crystallizes an important quality about a relationship in the way a joke only can:[16]

Their relationship consisted
In discussing if it existed.

If the micropoem takes the direct route to meaning, it also takes a direct route for delivering startling imagery. Just as all extraneous "fat" is boiled off the micropoem, all extraneous material is boiled off the imagistic micropoem, leaving a kernel of compelling image, as in Ezra Pound's famous "In a Station of the Metro":[17]

The apparition of these faces in the crowd;
Petals on a wet, black bough.

A short form that has lent itself particularly well to strong imagery has been the cinquain, developed by the American poet Adelaide Crapsey in the early 1900s. Inspired by Crapsey's reading of haiku and tanka, and designed to accommodate polysyllabic English, the cinquain is a five-line poem consisting of twenty-two syllables: two syllables in the first and

16. Thom Gunn, "Jamesian." *Poetry in Motion: 100 Poems from the Subways and Buses*, eds. Molly Peacock, Elise Paschen, and Neil Neches (New York & London: W. W. Norton, 1996): 89.
17. Ezra Pound, "In a Sation of the Metro." *Selected Poems* (New York: New Directions Books, 1957): 35.

last lines, and four, six and eight in the middle three lines. Many of Crapsey's cinquains feature haunting imagery, as in "Night Winds":[18]

> The old
> Old winds that blew
> When chaos was, what do
> They tell the clattered trees that I
> Should weep?

Vivid images have always been a hallmark of micropoems, as this next poem, written by Abu-l-Hasan Ali Ben Hisn in medieval Spain, demonstrates:[19]

> The wine pierced by sunlight reddens
> the fingers of the water carrying it,
> as the antelope's nose is stained by juniper.

Sound poems—and more generally, sense poems—also lend themselves to the very short form. This may be because many micropoems portray moments that can be conjured effectively by turning to the senses. A poem that describes

---

18. Adelaide Crapsey. *Three Centuries of American Poetry*, eds. Allen Mandelbaum and Robert D. Richardson, Jr. (New York: Bantam Books, 1999): 525.

19. Abu-l-Hasan Ali Ben Hisn, "The Glow of Wine." Tr. from Arabic to Spanish by Emilio García Gomez. Tr. Robert Bly. *The Sea and the Honeycomb: A Book of Tiny Poems*, ed. Robert Bly (Boston: Beacon Press, 1971): 8.

more than a moment—a long conversation, a love affair—of course employs the senses, but must move beyond these to convey the totality of the experience. Alan Pizzarelli epitomizes a typical summer afternoon:[20]

buzzZ
   slaP
buzzZ

E. E. Cummings does the same with the orgasm:[21]

n w
 O
 h
 S
LoW
 h
myGODye
 s s

In addition to existing as independent poems, micropoems have also functioned as units of longer "linked-verse" forms. For example, the Japanese renga, and its modern counterpart, renku, is a

20. Alan Pizzarelli, "buzzZ." *The Haiku Handbook: How to Write, Share, and Teach Haiku*, William J. Higginson and Penny Harter (Tokyo: Kodansha International, 1989): 69.
21. E. E. Cummings. *Complete Poems: 1904–1962*, ed. George J. Firmage (New York: Liveright, 1994): 1031.

collaborative poem written by several poets in alternating stanzas of seventeen and fourteen syllables. While the stanzas aren't considered independent poems, they consistently jump in different directions, always shifting while still linking. As a result, the reader can take each stanza as an independent poem.

Another linked-verse form where the units are independent is the ghazal, which is becoming better known in the United States in part because of the popularity of the Sufi poet Rumi. The ghazal is composed of a number of couplets that stand on their own as well as comprise the larger poem. Like the renga or renku, the substance of the couplets can be so different that a "leap" occurs in context and meaning between couplets. A ghazal by Agha Shahid Ali, relating the experience of exile of an Arabic-language writer, shows the leap:[22]

> The sky is stunned, it's become a ceiling of stone.
> I tell you it must weep. So kneel, pray for rain in
>   Arabic.
>
> At an exhibition of miniatures, such delicate
>   calligraphy:
> Kashmiri paisleys tied into the golden hair of
> _____Arabic!

22. Agha Shahid Ali, "Ghazal." *The Country Without a Post Office* (New York and London: W. W. Norton, 1997): 73.

The range of micropoems also includes the work of poets as diverse as Cid Corman, Aram Saroyan, Dick Higgins, the traditions of concrete poetry and even much poetry for children. Surveying some of the varieties of micropoems and their different cultural origins, it might seem impossible to characterize them as a group. However, micropoems as a class exhibit certain distinct qualities. The first, ironically, is a sense of space.

> The youth walks up to the white horse, to put
>   its halter on
> and the horse looks at him in silence.
> They are so silent they are in another world.
>   —D. H. Lawrence[23]

> Going to sleep, I cross my hands on my chest.
> They will place my hands like this,
> it will look as though I'm flying into myself.
>   —Saint Geraud[24]

Lawrence's "The White Horse" and Saint Geraud's "Death" both exhibit a certain vastness. Why the sense of space? Maybe because micropoems leave much unsaid. Robert Bly writes: "In the brief poem, it is all different: the poet takes the reader

23. D. H. Lawrence, "The White Horse." *The Sea and the Honeycomb: A Book of Tiny Poems*, ed. Robert Bly (Boston: Beacon Press, 1971): 7.
24. Saint Geraud, "Death." *The Sea and the Honeycomb: A Book of Tiny Poems*, ed. Robert Bly (Boston: Beacon Press, 1971): 54.

to the edge of a cliff, as a mother eagle takes its nestling, and then drops him. Readers with a strong imagination enjoy it, and discover they can fly. The others fall down to the rocks where they are killed instantly."[25]

The second quality of most micropoems is a sense of truth. Reading micropoems, one often feels that the poem is dispensing a truth (providing the poem fulfills its mission). It may be argued that all poetry does this, but perhaps this is even more pronounced in micropoems. Longer poetry usually has a narrative, prepatory material, or a sense of subjectivity that is less apparent in short poems even when they are overtly subjective. You sense that you are getting an experience of a truth in its purest and most unadulterated form, without the base alloys of story and narrative. This impression might also be due to the similarity of micropoems with proverbs and epigrams. Readers might be accustomed to learning "truths" in a short, direct format.

The third quality is a sense of concreteness. In longer poems, the truth or lesson that the poem imparts can be submerged within multiple layers: narrative, imagery, and so on. In micropoems, the truth is close to the surface; there is little room

25. Robert Bly, ed., "Dropping the Reader." *The Sea and the Honeycomb: A Book of Tiny Poems* (Boston: Beacon Press, 1971): x.

to conceal the lesson (if there is one), though the micropoem may also have multiple layers. This may be why one feels, paradoxically, that you sometimes get more out of a short poem than a long one. While lengthier poems may offer not only the "lesson" but also use other devices, the micropoem gives you the truth and not much else in an intuitive or imagistic package. It's easier for the reader to digest the truth when it is offered without costume. This is why proverbs tend to be succinct.

An artist's mission is to ask questions and to seek answers. If the world seems stormy and chaotic, it is art's job to act as an anchor. By offering a truth—even if that truth is contradictory or unnerving—art is a line of defense against life's confusion. Maybe the greatest quality of the micropoem is its kernelized clarity or wisdom; the micropoem is the eye of the storm:

> A man said to the universe:
> "Sir, I exist!"
> "However," replied the universe,
> "The fact has not created in me
> A sense of obligation."
> —Stephen Crane[26]

---

26. Stephen Crane, "A Man Said to the Universe." *Poetry in Motion: 100 Poems from the Subways and Buses*, eds. Molly Peacock, Elise Paschen, and Neil Neches (New York & London: W. W. Norton, 1996): 59.

SHORT POEMS: NOTHING TO TAKE AWAY

Reflecting upon industrial design, Antoine de Saint-Exupéry wrote, "In anything at all, perfection is finally attained not when there is no longer anything to add, but when there is no longer anything to take away, when a body has been stripped down to its nakedness."[1]

There are many kinds of short poems, from epigrams to haiku to imagistic shorts. A key characteristic (and pleasure) of the very short poem is, in Saint-Exupéry's words, its "stripped down" composition.

> The niche narrows
> Hones one thin
> Until his bones
> Disclose him

In Samuel Menashe's poem,[2] the lines are narrow and the words are short and monosyllabic. The thin "i" sound is one of the two primary assonances. The "m" and "n" sounds close the lines tight. The result is a poem that feels lean and compact, and, of course, dovetails perfectly with the subject matter.

---

1. Antoine de Saint-Exupéry, "Wind, Sand and Stars," in *Airman's Odyssey* (New York: Reynal & Hitchcock, 1942), 39.
2. Samuel Menashe, *New and Selected Poems* (New York: The Library of America, 2005), 166.

In *Snake Poems*, Francisco Alarcón employs a similar pared-down style:[3]

corn stalks
are upright
snakes

corn ears
rattle
in the wind

Like Menashe, Alarcón uses very short lines, monosyllabic words, and firm consonants. Substantively, Alarcón's poem is even narrower than that of Menashe; it comes closer to recording only what is essential. The first stanza takes the form of a definition, an equation where a = b: "a" being the subject and "b" being the image. He does the same in the poem entitled "Birds":[4]

snakes
in flight

This three-word poem is so direct that it may be regarded as even simpler than a definition. It may be seen as a designation, a label. In this way, it illustrates

3. Francisco X. Alarcón, *Snake Poems: An Aztec Invocation* (San Francisco: Chronicle Books, 1992), 67.
4. Ibid., 49.

the principle that Roland Barthes attributed to the short form of haiku: "the haiku diminishes to the point of pure and sole designation."[5]

The definition poem is similar in spirit to traditional short forms like the aphorism and proverb-poem. In these forms, there is little extraneous material; they often articulate only what is essential; and the language is unvarnished. Antonio Machado's proverb-poems are good examples.

> It is good knowing that glasses
> are to drink from;
> the bad thing is not to know
> what thirst is for.[6]

The same is true for related forms like the epigram and the riddle. These poems distill an essence—whether, say, a story or moral lesson—and at the same time are often formally pared-down, too.

It's important to remember, however, that the short poem doesn't always employ a minimalist style. Very brief poems—even pieces composed of a line or two—can feel lush and full.

---

5. Roland Barthes, *Empire of Signs*, trans. Richard Howard (New York: Hill and Wang, 1982), 83.
6. Antonio Machado, *Times Alone: Selected Poems of Antonio Machado*, tr. Robert Bly (Hanover, New Hampshire: Wesleyan University Press, 1983), 111.

The apparition of these faces in the crowd;
Petals on a wet, black bough.[7]

Though Ezra Pound's famous poem contains only one primary image, the poem is visually rich. While it is certainly stripped-down—in that it is two lines and communicates one central message—its voice is very different from those of the previously mentioned poems by Menashe and Alarcón. The following poem by Anna Akhmatova, slightly longer, is like Pound's in this way:

> He loved three things:
> White fowls, evensong,
> And antique maps of America.
>
> He hated the crying of children,
> Raspberry jam at tea,
> And female hysteria.
>
> And I was his wife.[8]

Akhmatova is able to describe the essence of the husband with a few compact lines. The language—with references to "antique maps" and

7. Ezra Pound, "In a Station of the Metro," *Selected Poems* (New York: New Directions Books, 1957), 35.
8. Anna Akhmatova, "He Loved Three Things," in *The Rag and Bone Shop of the Heart*, trans. Jerome Bullitt, ed. Robert Bly, James Hillman, and Michael Meade (New York: HarperPerennial, 1982), 268.

"raspberry jam"—is earthy and grounded. Both Akhmatova's poem and that of Pound are full-bodied: textually layered, dense and rich, evidence that it's important not to conflate the short poem with a stylistic minimalism.

Achieving the stripped-down perfection praised by Saint-Exupéry, whether minimalist or not, is no easy task. What Barthes observed about haiku is true of short forms generally: "The haiku has this rather fantasmagorical property: that we always suppose we ourselves can write such things easily."[9] Of course, truly great short poems are enormously difficult to pull-off. As Thomas McGrath jokes in his poem, "For a Critic Who Tries to Write Poems":

> Well, well, little poet!
> Still looking for a dew drop
> In the middle of a thunderstorm![10]

9. Roland Barthes, *Empire of Signs*, trans. Richard Howard (New York: Hill and Wang, 1982), 69.

10. Thomas McGrath, "For a Critic Who Tries to Write Poems," in *Passages Toward the Dark* (Port Townsend: Copper Canyon Press, 1982), 71.

ACKNOWLEDGMENTS

I would like to thank the editors and publishers of the following journals, books, and websites in which the poems in this collection first appeared:

A Hundred Gourds, Acorn, Frogpond, Mariposa, Modern Haiku, The Red Moon Anthologies, A New Resonance 6, The Haiku Foundation, My Neighbor: Two Autumns, Shiki Online Kukai, Raw Nervz, San Francisco Bay Guardian, moocat, Snapshot Press eChapbook Awards anthology, The Sacred in Contemporary Haiku, The Haiku Calendar 2010, Now This: Contemporary Poems of Beginnings, Renewals, and Firsts; The Temple Bell Stops: Contemporary Poems of Grief, Loss and Change.

My thanks to the judges and publishers of the following contests in which several of the poems won awards: HPNC Chime Award, Gerald Brady Senryu Contest, Anita Sadler Weiss Awards, Turtle Light Press Competition.

Special thanks to Sue Antolin for her feedback on this manuscript and to Jim Kacian for editing and production guidance. I want to express my gratitude to many haiku poets for advice and words of encouragement, including: Garry Gay, Fay Aoyagi, Carolyn Hall, Renée Owen, Bruce Feingold, Paul Miller, Joseph Robello, Patrick Gallagher, and Michael Sheffield. The same goes for my friends in the wider poetry world, especially: Keith Ekiss, Christopher Bernard, Jeanne Powell, Ho Lin, and John Nardizzi.

Essays

The essays in this book appeared first in the following journals:

"The Sword of Cliché." *Frogpond* 34:1. Reprinted and translated in *Haiku Reality* Vol. 8, No. 15.

"The Uses of Roots." *Frogpond* 36:1. Selected for *fear of dancing: The Red Moon Anthology of English-Language Haiku 2013*.

"The Uses of Foreign Words." *Frogpond* 37:2. Based on a paper presented at Haiku Pacific Rim, 2012.

"Two-Line Haiku." *Frogpond* 38:3.

"The Twin Pleasures of Kigo." *Mariposa* 30. (A shorter version of the essay appeared in *Mariposa*.)

"The 'Ancient Enemy.'" *Modern Haiku* 41.1.

"Leaping Haiku." *Mariposa* 9

"*Moonlight Changing Direction*: 'Introduction.'" Two Autumns Press.

"*The Half-Finished Bridge*: 'Introduction.'" Two Autumns Press.

"J. D. Salinger and Haiku." *Frogpond* XXIX:2. Selected for *big sky: The Red Moon Anthology of English-Language Haiku 2006*.

"The Trickster." *Chrysanthemum*—Issue 1.

"Glossy Black Painting." *Mariposa* 13. Selected for *dust of summers: The Red Moon Anthology of English-Language Haiku 2007*.

"The Inspiration of a Moment." *Frogpond* XXX:1.

"Simple Ingredients." *Simply Haiku* (Winter 2011).

"Short Poems: Nothing To Take Away." *The Cortland Review* (Issue 34 - February 2007).

"The Eye of the Storm." Selected for *Tundra: Journal of the Short Poem* (now defunct).

The following appear as posts on the *Religio* discussion forum on The Haiku Foundation website: (http://www.thehaikufoundation.org/forum_sm/index.php?topic=17.0): "Notes on Taoism and Haiku, Unity, Mystery, Grace, Ritual, Haiku as Prayer."

ABOUT THE AUTHOR

DAVID GRAYSON has been writing haiku since 1998. He joined the Haiku Poets of Northern California in 2002 and served as President and Vice President. He was Editor of two editions of the Two Autumns book series: *Moonlight Changing Direction* in 2008 and *The Half-Finished Bridge* in 2014 (which was short-listed for the 2014 Touchstone Awards). He was a featured poet in the 2009 Two Autumns book, *My Neighbor* as well as in *A New Resonance 6: Emerging Voices in English-Language Haiku*. Since 2010, he has been writing and moderating *Religio*, a forum on The Haiku Foundation website. He lives in the San Francisco Bay Area. This is his first full-length collection.